Pressure P

by
Michael Patrick

Copyright © 2005

All rights reserved

No part of this book or manuscript may be reproduced or transmitted in any form or by any means, electronic or mechanical, including photocopying, recording, or by any information storage and retrieval system, without permission in writing from the author.

If you do decide to copy this work, Master Patrick will come and demonstrate each and every technique upon you in person with full power…

Neither the author nor the publisher of this book is responsible in any manner whatsoever for any injury which may result from the use of the information or techniques contained within. Application of this science can be extremely hazardous and dangerous. The reader is encouraged to seek professional supervision and training before attempting to use any of the information contained herein. Death, disability, and severe injury temporary or permanent may result from application of this knowledge. The author, publisher, and distributors of this book hereby disclaim any liability from damages or injuries of any type which may result. **This book is for academic purposes only!**

Table of Contents

Credits v

Dedication vi

Preface ix

Chapter 1: The Heart Meridian 1

Chapter 2: The Pericardium Meridian 13

Chapter 3: The Triple Burner Meridian 27

Chapter 4: The Small Intestine Meridian 49

Chapter 5: The Lung Meridian 67

Chapter 6: The Large Intestine 81

Chapter 7: The Liver Meridian 97

Chapter 8: The Gall Bladder Meridian 113

Chapter 9: The Spleen Meridian 145

Chapter 10: The Stomach Meridian 165

Chapter 11: The Kidney Meridian 199

Chapter 12: The Bladder Merdiain 223

Chapter 13: The Conception Vessel 263

Chapter 14: The Governing Vessel 283

Chapter 15: The Yin Heel Vessel 303

Chapter 16: The Yang Heel Vessel 305

Chapter 17: The Yin Linking Vessel 307

Chapter 18: The Yang Linking Vessel 309

Chapter 19: The Penetrating Vessel 311

Chapter 20: The Girdle Vessel 315

Chapter 21: The Connecting Vessels 317

Appendix 321

Bibliography 341

About the Author 343

Credits

Acupuncture point diagrams contributed by Dragon Society International.

Cover design and other graphics by Mike Patrick.

Dedication

I want to take the time to thank those who have been there for me over the years. First and foremost, I want to thank the Lord Jesus Christ for being my Savior and all that He does for my family and me. I want to thank my parents Lawrence and Brenda Patrick, and George and Judy Wrenn; my wife Kasi; our children: Mark, Kayla, and Kristopher; my instructors: Grand Master Rick Moneymaker, Grand Master Tom Muncy, Grand Master Allen Wheeler, Sensei Max Jones; my Black Belts: Bill Adams, Danny McQueen, Gene Buxton, Joe Cronin, Benji Cox, Garrett Gross, David Ottinger, and Gene Maddox, who have allowed me to conduct my research on them other the years; my fellow instructors and friends with Dragon Society International; and finally to you for taking the time to read this book. You and so many more have greatly influenced me and encouraged me for so long. Thank you!

I am profoundly thankful to Grand Masters Rick Moneymaker and Tom Muncy, founders of Dragon Society International, for their guidance and influence over the last several years of working with them.

I would like to give a special thank you to Grand Master Allen Wheeler for all of his guidance and inspiration in the Martial Arts, especially in Isshinryu Karate. He is a wonderful man whom I respect greatly.

I would like to thank Sensei Max Jones who was my first Karate teacher. If it were not for him, I would not have even begun my studies of the Martial Arts. His attention to detail has aided my studies well.

Thank you to the Dragon Society International for the use of some of the acupuncture diagrams and other graphics. Their help allowed me to complete the book in a much shorter period of time than would have otherwise been possible.

Preface

This Atlas of Pressure Points details each and every point on the meridians and the effects of striking the points. This should prove useful in your studies as you learn what happens when these points are struck and how the opponent's energetic system is affected. You will also be able to do your own experimentation and learn which points are most active.

Please exercise caution. I have tried to convey the dangers of striking some of the more potent points. Much of this knowledge is from either direct experience or has been passed down from my instructors. Please assume that the points are capable of all that they are said to be and more. Several of the points, due to their physical location, may be fatal if struck due to the physiology of the body at that point alone, not including the energetic possibilities. Use extreme caution in your studies!

I hope that you will find this material useful for years to come.

Chapter 1

The Heart Meridian

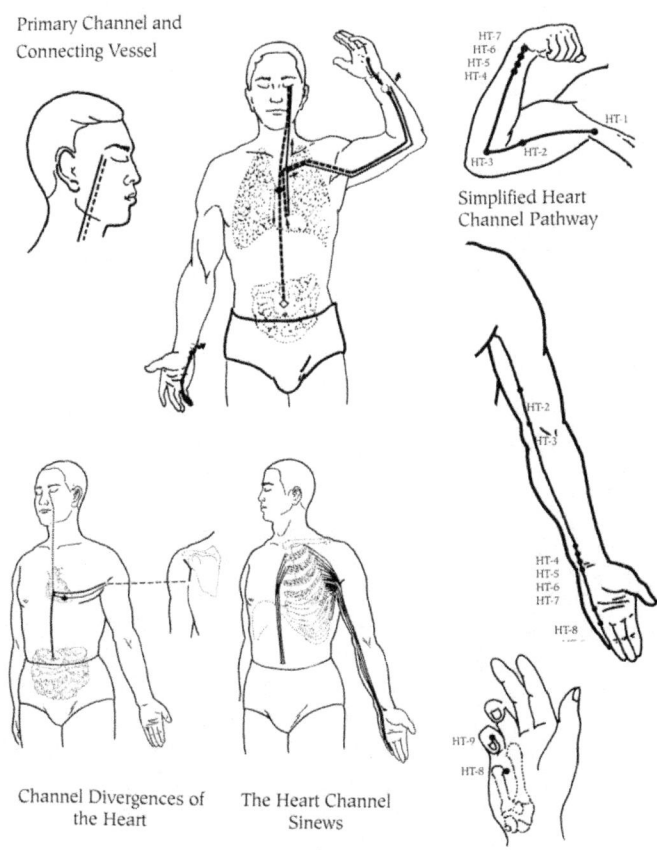

Primary Channel and Connecting Vessel

Simplified Heart Channel Pathway

Channel Divergences of the Heart

The Heart Channel Sinews

Heart Meridian Overview	
Element	Fire
This element creates	Earth
This element attacks	Metal
Polarity	Yin / Organ
Coupled Meridian	Small Intestine
Connecting Points	HT-5 & SI-4
Active Time	11:00 am to 1:00 pm
Entry Point	HT-1
Exit Point	HT-9
Sedation Point	HT-7
Tonification Point	HT-9
Alarm Point	CV-14
Associated Point	BL-15
Source Point	HT-7
Horary Point	HT-8
Wood / Well Point	HT-9
Fire / Spring Point	HT-8
Earth / Stream Point	HT-7
Metal / River Point	HT-4
Water / Sea Point	HT-3

GREATER VESSEL: From the Heart one vessel descends down to connect with the small intestine. A second branch ascends along the esophagus then crosses the face and cheek to connect with tissue surrounding the eye, while a third branch traverses the lungs to emerge from the axilla at HT-1 where it travels along the medial volar aspect of the arm and forearm to terminate at the radial corner of the fifth digit.

TENDINO MUSCULAR MERIDIAN: From HT-9 follows the Heart meridian to HT-1 (gathering points at HT-7, HT-3) and crosses widely across the chest to the midline and sends a small branch down to the umbilicus.

DIVERGENT CHANNEL (DISTINCT MERIDIAN): HT-1, SI-10 to BL-1 passing via the Heart and throat

LONGITUDINAL LUO CHANNEL: From Tongli HT-5 connects with the Small Intestine meridian and follows the Heart Meridian to the Heart zang then continues to the root of the tongue and the eye.

TRANSVERSE LUO CHANNEL: HT-5 to SI-4

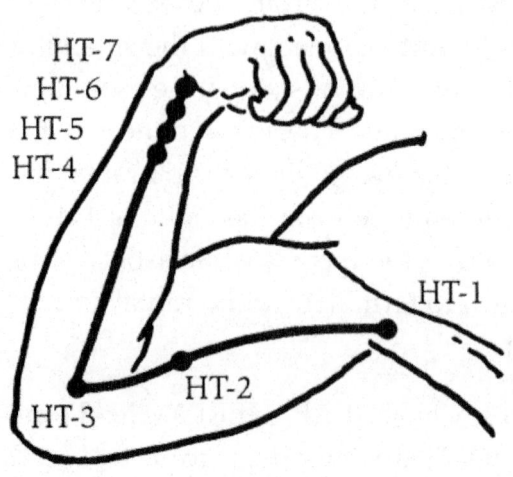

HT-1: *Iquan* (Summit's Spring)

In the center of the axilla, on the medial side of the axillary artery, at the lateral, inferior margin of the pectorals major muscle and in its deep position the point lies in the coracobrachialis muscle.

- Entry Point

- One of 36 Vital Points Listed in the Bubishi

This is a very dangerous heart point. A strike may cause the heart to stop instantly with even a medium to heavy strike. The point lies directly over the axillary artery. Because of this, massive artery damage can also be done when this point is struck. Brain function may also be affected with speech being impaired and mental activity, in general, having the potential to be severely affected. The emotional state of the person being struck may also be damaged.

In addition, localized shoulder damage may be done as well. This point is traditionally used to cure 'frozen shoulder' because of its ability to clear both external and internal *qi* of the meridian.

Activation angle: 90°

HT-2: *Ingling* (Youthful Spirit)

When the elbow is flexed, the point is 3 cun above the medial end of the transverse cubital crease, HT-3, in the groove medial to the biceps brachii.

Manipulation of this point may slow the heart rate enough to make one feel ill. This point also serves as an excellent nerve point strike affecting the whole arm and may even shock the upper body as well. With sufficient power, a knock out may be performed using this point.

Activation angle: 90°

HT-3: *Haohai* (Lesser Sea)

When the elbow is flexed, the point is at the medial end of the transverse cubital crease, in the depression anterior to the medial epicondyle of the humerus, in the pronator teres and the brachialis muscles.

- Uniting-He Point
- Water Point
- Destructive Point

This is a very dangerous point. It may cause the heart to stop if struck with the sufficient amount of power. It is a Water and He Sea point. It may have the immediate effect of stopping the heart. Since it lies over various tendons, it may cause damage to the tendon system.

This point is usually used to treat, among other things, stress, depression and emotional disturbances. A strike may also have the effect of causing long term nervous and emotional disorders.

This strike will unbalance the yin/yang relationship throughout the whole body. If this point is struck in a proximal way, it may cause high blood pressure; if it is struck straight in, it may cause the heart to weaken over a period of time.

Activation angle: 45

HT-4: *Ingdao* (Spirit's Path)

On the radial side of the tendon of the muscle flexor carp ulnaris, 1.5 cun above the transverse crease of the wrist when the palm faces upwards.

- River-jing Point
- Metal Point

This point is usually used for localized problems in healing. Manipulation of this point adds Fire to the heart and may cause high blood pressure.

Activation angle: 90°

HT-5: *Ongli* (Reaching the Measure)

When the palm faces upwards, the point is on the radial side of the tendon of the flexor carpi ulnaris muscle, 1 cun above the transverse crease of the wrist, between the tendon of the flexor carpi ulnaris and the flexor digitorum superficialis manus muscle, in its deep position, in the flexor digitorum sublimis muscle.

- Connecting-luo Point of the Small Intestine
- One of 36 Vital Points Listed in the Bubishi

This is a classic *qi* drainage point. It also works extremely well as a set up point strike. This point is used in acupuncture to effect qi drainage. In fact acupuncturists will not work this point too much since it could cause knock out due to *qi* drainage. This point may be used in conjunction with TB-12, where a strike may weaken the elbow greatly.

Activation angle: 90°

HT-6: *Inxi* (Yin Accumulation)

On the radial side of the tendon of flexor carp! ulnaris muscle, 0.5 cun above the transverse crease of the wrist.

- Nourishes the Blood
- Cleft-xi Point

HT-4, HT-5, HT-6, and HT-7 lie very close to one another, making it difficult to only manipulate one of these. Therefore, it is common that all four points are attacked together with a grabbing and/or shaking motion. This may cause great *qi* loss and immobilization. HT-6 is the Xi-Cleft point.

Activation angle: 90°

HT-7: *Henmen* (Spirit's Door)

On the transverse crease of the wrist, in the articular region between the pisform bone and the ulna, in the depression on the radial side of the tendon of the muscle flexor carpi ulnaris.

- Source Point
- Stream-shu Point
- Earth Point
- Nourishes the Blood
- Sedation Point

This point is known to have a great effect upon the *shen*, or the spirit. It is an Earth, *Yuan* and *Shu* point. A strike may damage the *shen's* emotional control over the body. The Fire element may then become unbalanced, thus causing too much heat to enter into the system, making the whole system become emotionally unstable and tense.

Activation angle: 90°

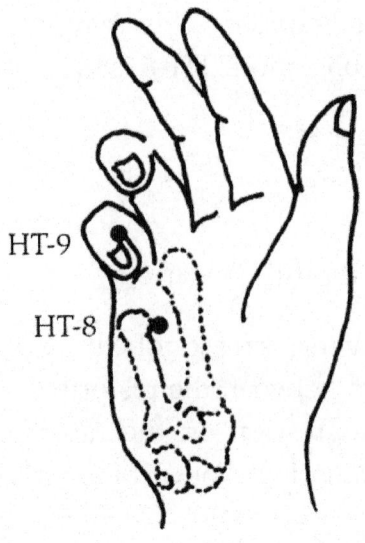

HT-8: *Haofu* (Lesser Residence)

On the palmar surface, between the 4th and 5th metacarpal bones. When the hand is supine and the fingers cupped in a half fist, this point is found on the palm just below the tip of the little finger. Between the fourth and fifth metacarpal bones, in the 4th lumbrical muscle and the tendon of the flexor digitorum sublimis muscle, in its deep position in the interosseous muscle.

- Spring-ying Point
- Fire Point
- Horary Point

This point may also upset the *shen* and the body's emotional stability. It is a Fire and *yong* point. When struck, it may upset the heart *qi*, causing the heart to be damaged. It may also upset the body's "time clock" creating symptoms of jet lag.

Activation angle: 90°

HT-9: *Haochong* (Lesser Pouring)

On the radial side of the little finger, about 0.1 cun posterior to the corner of the nail.

- Well-jing Point
- Wood Point
- Tonification Point
- Exit Point

This point is very difficult to use in combat. As such, it is normally used in the healing area as an emergency point or revival point. It is a Wood and *cheng* point. This is an excellent point for healing the heart.

Activation angle: 15°

Chapter 2

The Pericardium Meridian

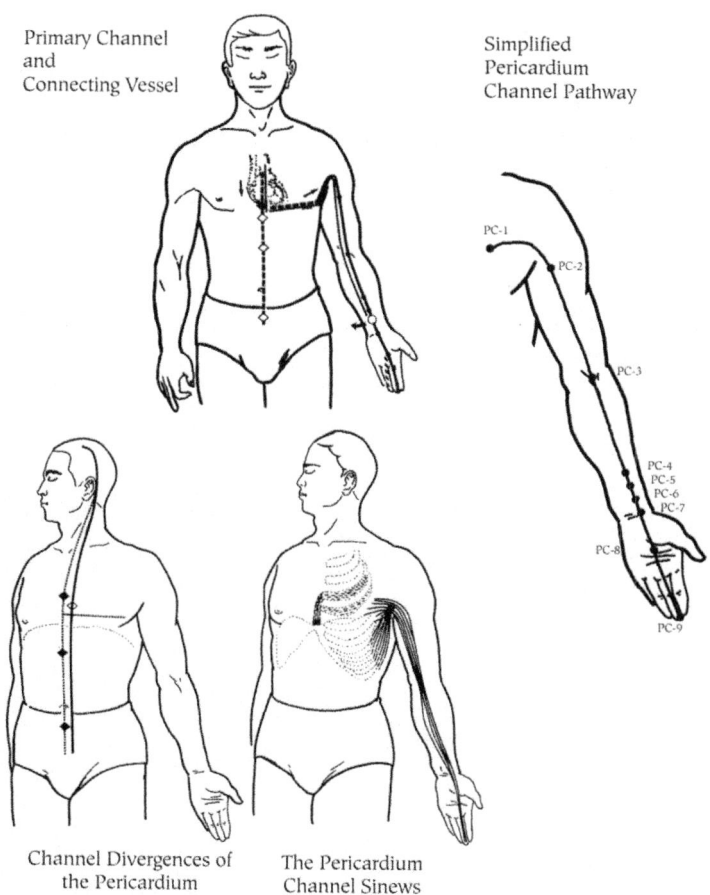

Primary Channel and Connecting Vessel

Simplified Pericardium Channel Pathway

Channel Divergences of the Pericardium

The Pericardium Channel Sinews

Pericardium Meridian Overview	
Element	Fire
This element creates	Earth
This element attacks	Metal
Polarity	Yin / Organ
Coupled Meridian	Triple Burner
Connecting Points	PC-6 & TB-4
Active Time	7:00 to 9:00 pm
Entry Point	PC-1
Exit Point	PC-8
Sedation Point	PC-7
Tonification Point	PC-9
Alarm Point	CV-17
Associated Point	BL-14
Source Point	PC-7
Horary Point	PC-8
Wood / Well Point	PC-9
Fire / Spring Point	PC-8
Earth / Stream Point	PC-7
Metal / River Point	PC-5
Water / Sea Point	PC-3

GREATER VESSEL: From the Heart one vessel descends down to connect with the small intestine. A second branch ascends along the esophagus then crosses the face and cheek to connect with tissue surrounding the eye, while a third branch traverses the lungs to emerge from the axilla at PC-1 where it travels along the medial volar aspect of the arm and forearm to terminate at the radial corner of the fifth digit.

TENDINO MUSCULAR MERIDIAN: From PC-9 follows the Heart meridian to PC-1 (gathering points at PC-7, PC-3) and crosses widely across the chest to the midline and sends a small branch down to the umbilicus.

DIVERGENT CHANNEL (DISTINCT MERIDIAN): PC-1, SI-10 to BL-1 passing via the Heart and throat

LONGITUDINAL LUO CHANNEL: From Tongli PC-5 connects with the Small Intestine meridian and follows the Heart Meridian to the Heart zang then
continues to the root of the tongue and the eye.

TRANSVERSE LUO CHANNEL: PC-6 to TB-4

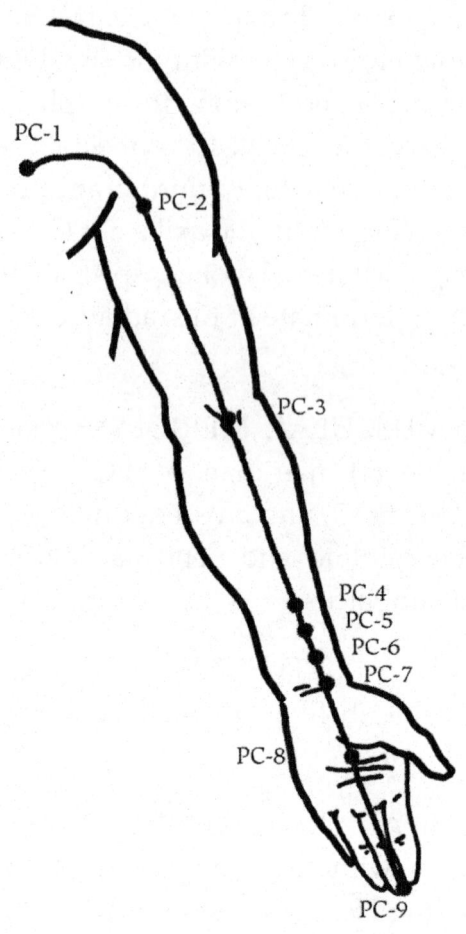

PC-1: *Tianchi* (Heavens Pool)

1 cun lateral to the nipple, in the 4th intercostal space.

Tian means heaven, *Chi* means pool, the point is lateral to the breast and the milk secreted from the breast of women is said to be like nectar from a heavenly pool.

- Origin Point of the Pericardium
- Entry Point
- Window of the Sky Point

PC-1 will affect the heart no matter whether it is struck on the left or right side of the body. It may also have an affect upon the lungs causing coughing and an itchy feeling in the neck. It may drain *qi* from the heart and lungs, causing significant damage to the entire energetic system.

This is the *mu* point of the pericardium meaning that it is an alarm point. It is also a Window of the Sky point. When this is used with SP-17, it may have devastating internal damage with little or no external damage visible. Death may occur when this combination is struck and may appear to be the result of a heart attack. This point has also been known to affect the kidneys as well.

Activation angle: 90°

PC-2: *Tianquan* (Heaven's Spring)

2 cun below the end of the anterior axillary fold, between the two heads of the biceps brachii muscle.

This point may also affect the heart and can be used in conjunction with LU-3 in a grab to cause great *qi* disruption and drainage. Localized pain and nerve damage may also be done. A strike to PC-2 can sometimes disrupt the breathing with the recipient exhaling and sinking at the same time.

Activation angle: 90°

PC-3: *Quze* (Crooked Marsh)

On the transverse cubital crease, at the ulnar side of the tendon of the biceps brachii muscle. Qu means curve and Ze means marsh, the *qi* of the meridian infuses into the shallow depression of the elbow like water flowing into a marsh.

- Uniting-He Point
- Water Point
- Destructive Point
- Downbears Counterflow

This is a Water and *He* point. Strikes may have an effect upon the heart and the intestines. It may also add heat to the heart causing long term medical conditions such as cold sores on the mouth and lips, babbling, etc. It may also affect the emotions, especially later in one's life.

PC-3 may drain energy and affect the heart when struck downward towards the wrist. It may also affect the lungs when struck slightly upward in the other direction.

Activation angle: 90°

PC-4: *Ximen* (Gate of the Crevice)

5 cun above the transverse crease of the wrist, on the line connecting PC-3 to PC-7, between the tendons of the palmaris longus and flexor carpi radialis muscles, in the flexor digitorumsuperficialis manus muscle. In its deep position in the flexor digitorum sublimus muscle.

- Cleft-xi Point

This point may affect the heart, especially if the recipient has existing heart conditions. In this case the heart may stop immediately following the strike. In other cases, it may cause the heart to become weaker, exposing it to external pathogenic attack.

The strike may be made more effective if PC-5 and PC-6 are also used. PC 4 is a Xie-cleft point which may cause the heart to become tense and its pulse increase for no apparent reason and thus causing high blood pressure. It may also have an effect upon the *shen*, or spirit.

Activation angle: 90°

PC-5: Jianshi (Intermediary)

3 cun above the transverse crease of the wrist, between the tendons of the muscles palmaris longus and flexor carpii radialis, in the flexor digitorum superficialis manus muscle. In its deep position in the flexor digitorum sublimis muscle.

- River-jing Point
- Metal Point
- Downbears counterflow

This is a Metal and *jing* point. It may have an effect upon the mind, causing scattered thinking and tension leading to mental illness. The heart may also be adversely affected by striking this point. The balance of the heart and lung may also be disturbed and drain *qi*. The heart may be stopped by striking this point in conjunction with PC-6 and PC-4. Digestion may also be impaired from striking this point.

Activation angle: 90°

PC-6: *Eiguan* (Inner Gate)

2 cun above the transverse crease of the wrist, between the tendons of the palmaris longus and flexor carpi radialis muscles, in the flexor digitorum superficialis manus muscle. In its deep position in the flexor digitorum sublimis muscle. *Nei* means "pass" and *guan* means "pass", this point is an important site on the medial aspect of the forearm, like a pass.

- Connecting-luo Point of the Triple Burner
- Confluence Point of Yin Linking Vessel
- Downbears counterflow
- Master Point of the Yin Linking Vessel
- Coupled Point with Extraordinary Meridian of the Penetrating Vessel

This is an amazing point. It is a connecting-*luo* point, a master point for *Yin Wei-Mai*, and a coupled point of *Chong Mai*. When struck, it often upsets the *yin/yang* balance of the body. It is one of the best points for *qi* drainage. This point can be incorporated into wrist locks using the fingers to dig into the point making the lock much easier to apply. This point may cause the heart to race for no apparent reason; respiration may also be increased in the lungs.

Activation angle: 90°

PC-7: *Daling* (Big Tomb)

In the depression in the middle of the transverse crease of the wrist, between the tendons of the palmaris longus and flexor carpi radialis muscles, and in the flexor hallucis longus muscle and the tendon of the flexor digitorum sublimis muscle. *Da* means "big or large" and *ling* means "tomb or mould." The protrusion of the palmar root is quite large, like a mould and the point is in the depression of the wrist proximal to it.

- Source Point
- Stream-shu Point
- Earth Point
- Downbears counterflow

- Sedation Point

This is an Earth, *yuan* and *shu* point. A strike here often has an immediate effect upon the heart and may shock it and make the body vulnerable to a more devastating strike. This point is often used as a set up point to other meridians such as the heart. It may cause too much heat to invade the heart.

Activation angle: 90°

PC-8: *Laogong* (Labor's Palace)

When the hand is placed palm upwards, the point is between the 2nd and 3rd metacarpal bones, proximal to the metacarpophalangeal joint, on the radial side of the 3rd metacarpal bone. With the fingers cupped in the palm in a half fist, this point can be found in front of the tip of the middle finger between the 2nd and 3rd metacarpal bones. Below the point are the aponeurosis, the 2nd lumbrical and the superficial and deep tendons of the flexor digitorum muscles. In its deep position are the origin of the transverse head of the adductor hallucis muscle and the interossei muscle. *Lao* means "labor" and *gong* means "center." The hand is for labor so here *lao* refers to the hand. The point is in the center of the palm.

- Spring-ying Point
- Fire Point
- Downbears counterflow
- Horary Point
- Exit Point

This is a Fire and *yong* point. When struck, heat is often experienced in the heart. This point is where *qi* emanates from the hand.

Activation angle: 90°

PC-9: *Zhongchong* (Middle Pouring)

In the center of the tip of the middle finger. Another location is 0.1 cun from the base of the middle fingernail on the radial side.

- Uniting-He Point
- Well-jing Point
- Wood Point
- Tonification Point

This is a healing point and probably should not be used in a self defense situation. It is a Wood and *cheng* point. As such, it is often used in emergency treatments such as coma and is usually bled.

Activation angle: 15°

Chapter 3

The Triple Burner Meridian

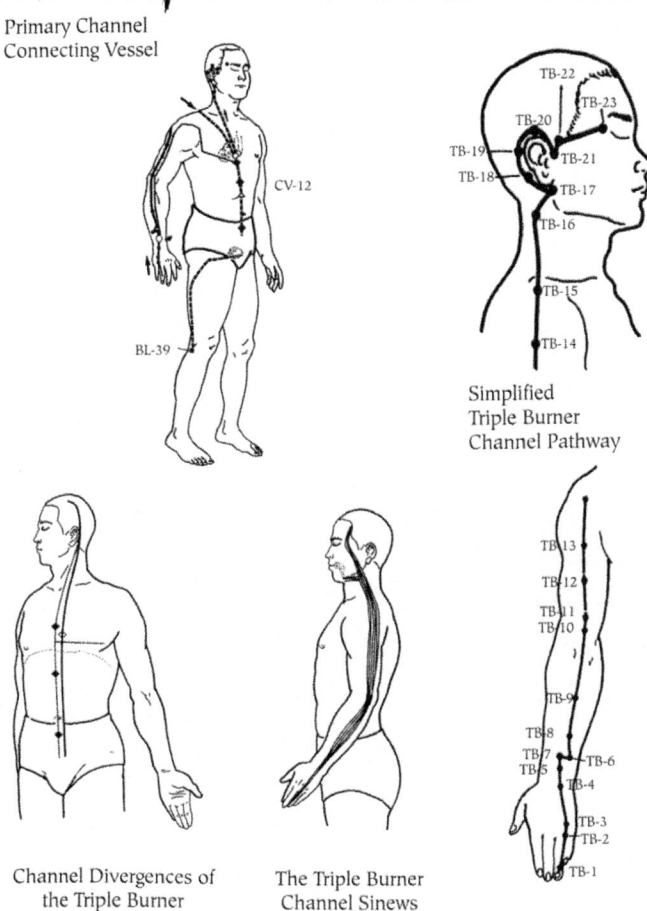

Primary Channel
Connecting Vessel

CV-12

BL-39

Simplified Triple Burner Channel Pathway

Channel Divergences of the Triple Burner

The Triple Burner Channel Sinews

Triple Burner Meridian Overview	
Element	Fire
This element creates	Earth
This element attacks	Metal
Polarity	Yang / Bowel
Coupled Meridian	Pericardium
Connecting Points	TB-5 & PC-7
Active Time	9:00 to 11:00 pm
Entry Point	TB-1
Exit Point	TB-23
Sedation Point	TB-10
Tonification Point	TB-3
Alarm Point	CV-5
Associated Point	BL-22
Source Point	TB-4
Horary Point	TB-6
Metal / Well Point	TB-11
Water / Spring Point	TB-10
Wood / Stream Point	TB-9
Fire / River Point	TB-8
Earth / Sea Point	TB-5

MAIN CHANNEL PATHWAY

The Triple Heater channel starts at the tip of the ring finger. Running between the 4th and 5th metacarpal bones, it flows to the wrist and up the lateral aspect of the arm between the radius and ulna. It then reaches the shoulder joint and the supraclivicular fossa from where it goes down to the chest to connect with the pericardium. It then descends through the diaphragm to the abdomen to join the middle and lower Burners.

From the chest, a branch goes up to the supraclavicular fossa from where it ascends to the neck and region behind the ear. It then turns downwards to the cheek and terminates in the infra-orbital region.

From behind the ear, a branch enters the ear, re-emerges in front of the ear and links with the Gall Bladder channel.

CONNECTING CHANNEL PATHWAY

The Connecting channel starts at Waiguan TB-5 and flows up the arm talong the main channel to the shoulder and chest where it links with the Pericardium channel.

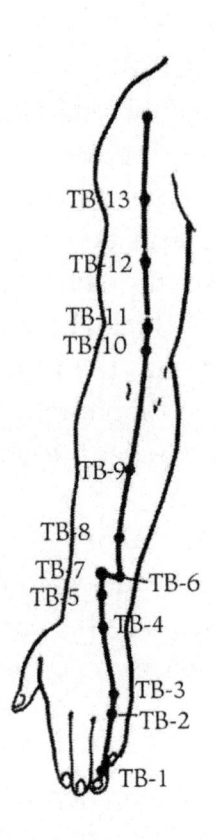

TB-1: *Guanchong* (Gate's Pouring)

On the lateral side of the ring finger, around 0.1 cun posterior to the corner of the nail. *Guan* here means "bend" as the ring finger cannot be stretched out alone. *Chong* means "gushing." The point is near the tip of the ring finger and is the *jing* well point where the *qi* of the meridian originates and gushes upwards along the channel.

- Well-jing Point

- Metal Point

  - Frees the channels, Quickens the Connecting Vessels

  - Entry Point

This point is often employed in the healing arts. It is rarely ever used in Martial Arts applications.

Activation angle: 15°

TB-2: *Emen* (Fluids Door)

Proximal to the margin of the web between the ring and small fingers. The point is located with a clenched fist.

- Frees the channels
- Quickens the Connecting Vessels
- Destructive Point
- One of 36 Vital Points Listed in the Bubishi

This point may cause internal damage to the body. It is also employed in locks.

This is a Water and *yong* point. When attacked, it may cause great *qi* disruption to the body, especially the movement of fluids throughout the system.

Activation angle: 90°

TB-3: *Hongzhu* (Middle Island)

When the hand is palm down, the point is on the dorsum of the hand between the 4th and 5th metacarpal bones, in the depression proximal to the metacarpophalangeal joint in the 4th interosseous muscle.

- Wood Point
- Stream-shu Point
- Frees the channels
- Quickens the Connecting Vessels
- Tonification Point

This is a Wood and *shu* point. The hearing may be affected when struck with sufficient power.

This point is often employed in finger locks.

Activation angle: 90°

TB-4: *Angchi* (Pool of Yang)

At the junction of the ulna and carpal bones, in the depression lateral to the tendon of extensor digitorum communis muscle. With the hand supline, this point can be found directly above the transverse crease on the dorsal side of the wrist, in a hollow above the 3rd and 4th metacarpal bones, between the tendons of extensor digitorum and extensor digiti minimi manus muscles.

- Source Point
- Frees the channels
- Quickens the Connecting Vessels

This point is a *yuan* point. It may cause damage to the tendons and to the *qi*. Some say that it is not good to be struck here if you have had either a vasectomy or had your uterus removed.

This point may cause great pain and *qi* to be drained. It is an excellent set up point.

Activation angle: 90°

TB-5: *Aiguan* (Outer Gate)

2 cun above TB-4, between the radius and ulna and extensor digitorum and extensor hallucis longus muscles.

- Connecting-luo Point of the Pericardium
- Confluence Point of Yang Linking Vessel
- Frees the channels
- Quickens the Connecting Vessels
- Regulates the Spleen and Stomach
- Master Point of the Yang Linking Vessel
- Coupled Point with Extraordinary Meridian of the Girdling Vessel

This point may cause the opponent to collapse. The drainage of *qi* is considerable. Pain is also incredible when struck with a smaller weapon. This is a *luo* point and a master point of *Yang Wei Mai*. This point is connected with many other meridians because of its linkage with the extraordinary vessels. It often unbalances the *yin* and *yang* of the body.

Activation angle: 90°

TB-6: *Higou* (Branch Supporting Ditch)

3 cun above TB-4, 1cun above TB-5, between the radius and ulna and the extensor digitorum and extensor hallucis longus muscles. With the palm down, the point is found on the radial side of the extensor digitorum muscle. *Zhi* means "limbs" and *gou* means "ditch." Here, *zhi* is referring to the upper limbs and the ditch is between the radius and ulna.

- Spring-ying Point
- Fire Point
- River-jing Point
- Water Point
- Frees the channels
- Quickens the Connecting Vessels
- Regulates the Spleen and Stomach
- Horary Point

This is a Fire and *jing* point. When struck, this point may cause intestinal problems. It often hinders the flow of *qi* throughout the body and causes heat to rise in the middle and upper burners; this may cause problems in the mind and breathing difficulties.

The strike will most likely cause intense pain and *qi* drainage and may cause the recipient to collapse. This point is most often employed as a set up point.

Activation angle: 90°

TB-7: *Uizong* (Meeting of the Clan)

3 cun proximal to the wrist, about 1 finger breadth lateral to TB-6 on the radial side of the ulna.

- Cleft-xi Point

This is a xi-cleft point (accumulation point). A strike to any xi-cleft point causes the *qi* to disperse in many directions effecting great *qi* disruption all throughout the body. As such, this point is an excellent set up point. Immediately, great pain may be felt at this point when manipulated.

Activation angle: 90°

TB-8: *Anyangluo* (Three Yang Connection)

4 cun above TB-4, between the radius and ulna and between the exterior digitorum and the origin of the abductor pollicis longus muscles.

A strike here may cause death, if it is of significant power, due to immediate *qi* drainage.

TB-9: *Idu* (Four Ditch)

When the hand is palm down, the point is 5 cun below the olecranon (elbow), between the radius and ulna and the extensor carpi ulnaris muscle of the forearm.

This is more of a nerve and muscular strike than an energetic strike, though it can cause *qi* drainage. It may cause temporary paralysis of the arm.

Activation angle: 90°

TB-10: *Ianjing* (Heaven's Well)

When the elbow is flexed, the point is in the depression about 1 cun superior to the olecranon of the elbow. In the cavity above the olecranon at the posterior aspect of the lower end of the humerus and the superior margin of the olecranon prominence of the ulna, in the tendon of the triceps muscle.

- Earth Point
- Uniting-He Point

- Frees the channels
- Quickens the Connecting Vessels
- Sedation Point

This is an Earth and *he* point. This point is connected with all three of the burners and may cause damage throughout the entire system of the body.

Activation angle: 90°

TB-11: *Inglengyuan* (Cooling Gulf)

Located 1 cun above TB-10.

This point is often used to weaken the elbow joint for a dislocation or break.

Activation angle: 90°

TB-12: *Iaoluo* (Melting Luo River)

On the line joining the olercranon and TB-14 mid way between TB-11 and TB-13.

The whole arm may be damaged. This point may be used as a set up point to drain *qi* from the entire body. It is often employed in arm locks, dislocations, and breaks.

When it is struck using an upward direction, it may cause a large amount of *qi* to be driven towards the head, creating the potential for a knock out.

Activation angle: 90°

TB-13: *Aohui* (Shoulders Meeting)

On the line joining the olercranon process from TB-10 to TB-14. It lies 3 cun below TB-14 in the depression on the posterior inferior aspect of the deltoid muscle.

- Intersection Point of the Bladder
- Origin Point of the Triple Burner

This point is a point along the *Yang Wei Mai* and can be used with other points to form devastating techniques.

It is also connected to LI-14. Striking these two points together would be very disastrous for the recipient.

Activation angle: 90°

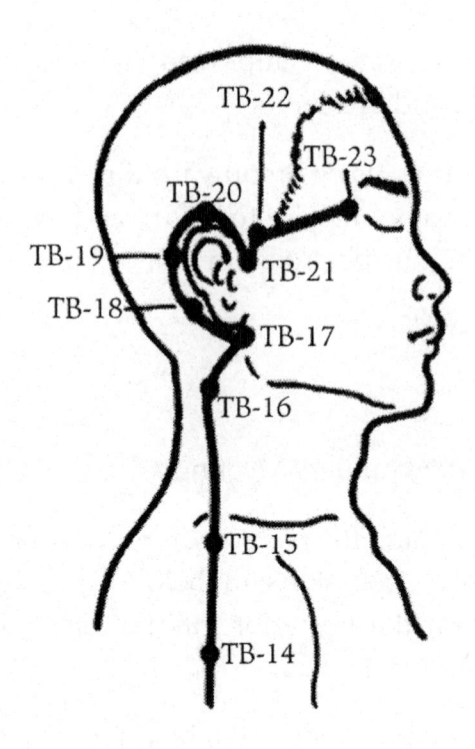

TB-14: *Ianliao* (Shoulder Seam)

Posterior and inferior to the acromion, in the depression about 1 cun posterior to LI-15. In the deltoid muscle. *Jian* means "shoulder" and *liao* means "foramen." This point lies is in a foramen on the shoulder.

- Intersection Point of the Bladder
- Origin Point of the Triple Burner

This is also a *Yang Wei Mai* point. Great scapular injury may occur with a nauseous feeling being caused by this point's relation to SI-12. This point has considerable physical protection and thus requires a penetrating strike to do damage.

Activation angle: 90°

TB-15: *Iianlao* (Heaven's Seam)

Midway between GB-21 and SI-13 on the superior angle of the scapula. *Tiao* means "heaven" and *you* means "foramen." Upper is referred to as heaven and the point is in a foramen above the shoulder blade.

- Origin Point of the Triple Burner
- Intersection Point of the Yang Motility vessel

This point is related to ST-12 and may cause the will to fight to be diminished. It may also harm the whole *qi* system of the body and can cause localized pain over the upper back area. It has also been known to cause a sick feeling in the stomach.

Activation angle: 90°

TB-16: *Ianyao* (Heaven's Window)

Posterior and inferior to the mastoid process, on the posterior border of the sternocleidomastoideus, level with SI-17, and BL-10. Near the hairline, in the posterior margin at the insertion of the sternocleidomastoid muscle.

- Window of the Sky Point

This point will cause a knock out alone. It may also cause death if it is struck hard.

It is a Window of the Sky point and so will have a great effect upon the brain by placing too much *yang qi* into the brain causing confusion or knock out.

Temporary emotional problems may also be experienced.

This point is extremely dangerous and should be avoided except for in life-threatening situations.

Activation angle: 90°

TB-17: *Ifeng* (Shielding Wind or Wind Screen)

Posterior to the lobule of the ear, in the depression between the mandible and mastoid process.

- Intersection Point of the Gall Bladder
- Origin Point of the Triple Burner
- Frees the channels
- Quickens the Connecting Vessels
- One of 36 Vital Points Listed in the Bubishi

A very dangerous point when struck properly. Moreover, this point can also be used as a controlling point and can cause the recipient to collapse or come-along with you.

Activation angle: 90°

TB-18: *Imai* (Feeding the Vessels)

In the center of the mastoid process, at the junction of the middle and lower thirds of the curve by TB-17 and TB-20, posterior to the helix at the root of the auricle.

This is also a very dangerous strike due to trauma to the brain. A hard strike here can cause death. A knock out will occur with a medium strike.

Activation angle: 90°

TB-19: *Uxi* (Skull's Rest)

Posterior to the ear, at the junction of the upper and middle thirds of the curve formed by TB-17 and TB-20, behind the helix or 1 cun above TB-18 behind the ear.

Can be fatal when combined with TB-18 and a hard blow. With a medium power strike, the recipient may be knocked out or totally disorientated at least due to the location of the point near the brain. You can easily strike both points with a palm strike.

Activation angle: 90°

TB-20: *Iaosun* (Angle of Regeneration)

Directly above the apex of the ear, within the hairline of the temple. *Jiao* means "corner" and *sun* means "reticular collateral." This point is on the temporal region corresponding to the ear apex, where the reticular meridians are distributed.

- Intersection Point of the Gall Bladder
- Origin Point of the Triple Burner
- Intersection Point of the Large Intestine

This point must be struck fairly hard to produce any effect. With hard strikes, extreme dizziness and fainting can result, followed by nausea. A knock may occur with a medium to hard power strike.

Activation angle: 90°

TB-21: *Ermen* (Ear's Door)

In the depression anterior to the supratragic notch and slightly superior to the condyloid process of the mandible. The point is located with the mouth open. *Er* means "ear" and *men* means "door." This point is in front of the ear, like a door to the ear.

- Frees the channels
- Quickens the Connecting Vessels

Strikes to this point may cause a feeling of illness that pervades the whole torso. Struck hard, it may cause knock out. This feeling may be transformed into pain, causing the recipient to feel like they are experiencing a heart attack.

Activation angle: 90°

TB-22: *Eliao* (Harmony's Seam)

Anterior and superior to TB-21, level with the auricle, on the natural hairline of the temple where the superficial temporal artery passes.

- Intersection Point of the Small Intestine
- Intersection Point of the Gall Bladder
- Origin Point of the Triple Burner

This point is very similar to TB-21. It may affect *qi* drainage. With a hard strike it may cause knock out. Using a palm strike to this point, you will also get a number of other points such as the Gall Bladder points in the area and thus cause death from the large number of points struck.

Activation angle: 90°

TB-23: *Sizhukong* (Silken Bamboo Hollow)

In the depression at the lateral end of the eyebrow, on the lateral border of the zygomatic process of the frontal bone, in the orbicularis oculi muscle. *Sizhu* means "slender bamboo" and *kong* means "space." The point is at the lateral end of the eyebrow, which looks like a slender bamboo and it is in a shallow depression.

- Frees the channels
- Quickens the Connecting Vessels
- Exit Point

This point is extremely dangerous and may cause knock out even at low power levels. A hard strike may cause death. This point often drains qi from the lower and middle burners.

Localized pain is felt at first, followed by a sinking feeling in the chest and abdomen as the qi is drained. Often, the knees will become weak and then knock out results. Even after the recipient has been revived, the legs remain shaky. When this point is struck slightly inwards towards the eye, blindness may result.

Activation angle: 15°

Chapter 4

The Small Intestine Meridian

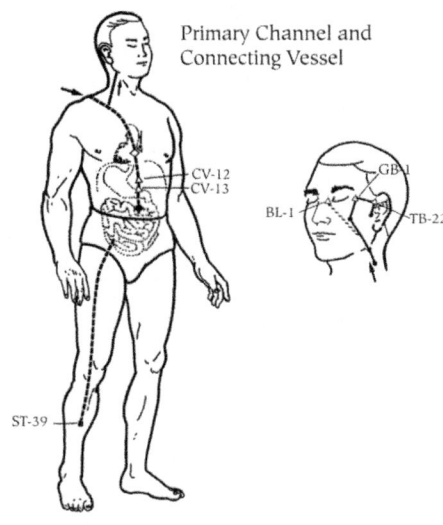

Primary Channel and Connecting Vessel

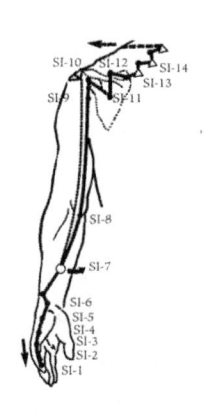

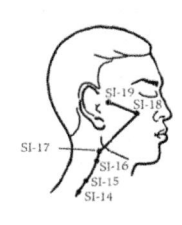

Simplified Small Intestine Channel Pathway

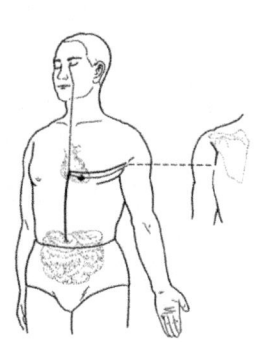

Channel Divergences of the Small Intestine

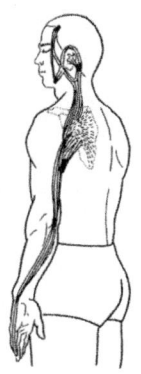

The Small Intestine Channel Sinews

Small Intestine Meridian Overview	
Element	Fire
This element creates	Earth
This element attacks	Metal
Polarity	Yang / Bowel
Coupled Meridian	Heart
Connecting Points	SI-7 & HT-7
Active Time	1:00 to 3:00 pm
Entry Point	SI-1
Exit Point	SI-19
Sedation Point	SI-8
Tonification Point	SI-3
Alarm Point	CV-4
Associated Point	BL-27
Source Point	SI-4
Horary Point	SI-5
Metal / Well Point	SI-1
Water / Spring Point	SI-2
Wood / Stream Point	SI-3
Fire / River Point	SI-5
Earth / Sea Point	SI-8
Meridian Connections	GV-14
	SI-3 (GV, Yang Heel)
	CV-12
	CV-13
	CV-17

GREATER VESSEL: From the ulnar side of the tip of the fifth finger, it runs along the ulnar side of the hand and arm to the ulnar groove, where it continues via LI-14 to the posterior scapular and supra spinal areas before ascending along the anterior aspect of the SCM and ending just in front of the ear. It connects with GV-14 and sends a branch via ST-12 down along the esophagus and stomach to the small intestine.

TENDINO MUSCULAR MERIDIAN: SI-1 to GB-13

DIVERGENT CHANNEL (DISTINCT MERIDIAN): SI-10, HT-1 TO ST-1 (BL-1)

LONGITUDINAL LUO CHANNEL: SI-7

TRANSVERSE LUO CHANNEL: SI-6 to HT-7

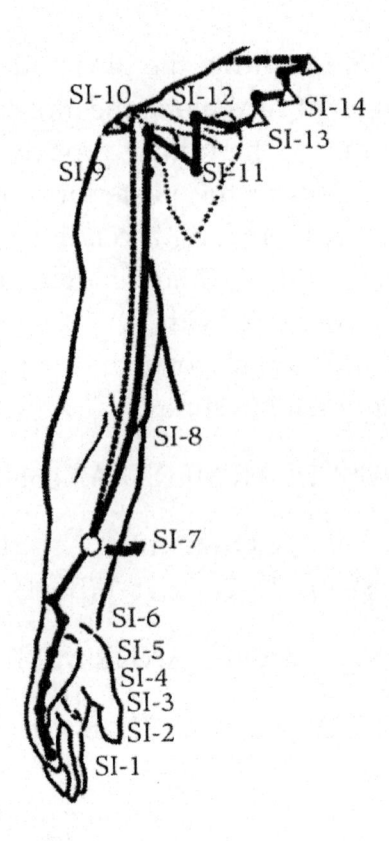

SI-1: *Haoze* (Lesser Marsh)

On the ulnar side of the little finger, about 0.1 cun posterior to the corner of the nail.

- Well-jing Point
- Metal Point
- Entry Point

This is a Metal and *cheng* point. It controls the muscle/tendon and divergent meridians. Striking this point may weaken the body's system over a long period of time. It may also cause the recipient to become very angry as heat invades the heart. This point is often used more in healing than in Martial Arts.

Activation angle: 15°

SI-2: *Iangu* (Forward Valley)

When a loose fist is made, the point is distal to the metacarpophalangeal joint, at the junction of the red and white skin.

- Spring-ying Point
- Water Point
- Destructive Point

This is a Water and *yong* point. A strike may cause heat to rise in the body and create all kinds of problems within the system. It is often employed in finger locks.

Activation angle: 45°

SI-3: *Ouxi* (Black Creek)

When a loose fist is made, the point is proximal to the head of the 5th metacarpal bone on the ulna side, in the depression at the junction of the red and white skin. Lateral to the abductor digiti minimi manus.

- Wood Point
- Stream-shu Point
- Confluence Point of Governing Vessel
- Tonification Point
- Master Point of the Governing Vessel
- Coupled Point with Extraordinary Meridian of the Yang Motility vessel

This is a Wood point, *shu* point, and a master point for the *Du Mai*. A strike here may cause an imbalance between 'heaven' and 'earth', or between the upper and lower body.

A strike may lead to the senses becoming confused and the nerves and tendons may tense; this would make this an excellent set up point for a lock.

This point may also have an adverse effect upon the liver, causing great pain and *qi* drainage to be evidenced.

Activation angle: 45°

SI-4: *Angu* (Wrist Bone)

On the ulna side of the palm, in the depression between the base of the 5th metacarpal bone and the triquetral bone. Lateral to the origin of the abductor digiti minimi manus.

- Source Point

It is a *yuan* point. This point is great for healing, but less so for Martial Arts applications. It may also affect the heart by causing heat to accumulate. It may also have an affect upon the bladder as well. Immediately, it will cause an energy loss and is a good point for control tactics.

Activation angle: 90°

SI-5: *Anggu* (Valley of Yang)

On the ulna side of the wrist, in the depression between the styloid process of the ulna and the triquetral bone.

- Fire Point
- River-jing Point

- Horary Point

This point is an excellent set up point. It is a Fire and *jing* point. A hard strike here has the ability to cause a build up of stagnant *Yang qi* in the head and may lead to madness.

Activation angle: 90°

SI-6: *Anglao* (Nurishing the Old)

Dorsal to the head of the ulna. When the palm faces the chest, the point is in the bony cleft on the radial side of the styloid process of the ulna. On the dorsal aspect of the ulna, above the head of the ulna at the wrist, between the tendons of the extensor carpi ulnaris and the extensor digiti minimi manus muscles.

- Cleft-xi Point

This is a xi-cleft point. A strike to this point may have adverse effects on the *qi; it may also* cause the tendons in the body to become tense. This point can also cause vision to falter and even instant temporary blindness.

Activation angle: 45°

SI-7: *Hizheng* (Branch of Uprightness)

5 cun proximal to the wrist, on the line joining SI-5 and SI-8.

- Connecting-luo Point of the Heart

This is a very dangerous point. It may increase the amount of *yang qi* in the heart causing nausea and fainting; it may also cause great immediate pain. It has been said that a strike to this point may cause permanent blindness over an extended period of time.

Activation angle: 90°

SI-8: *Iaohai* (Small Sea)

Between the olecranon of the ulna and the medial epicondyle of the humerus. The point is located with the elbow flexed.

- Earth Point
- Uniting-He Point
- Sedation Point

This is also a dangerous point. It may cause considerable pain and drain the *qi*. It is often struck in conjunction with LU-5, often causing knock out or even death. It is an Earth and *he* point.

This point is often applied in a controlling technique and may drop the opponent to the ground.

Activation angle: 90°

SI-9: *Ianzhen* (Shoulder Chastity)

Posterior and inferior to the shoulder joint. When the arm is adducted, the point is 1 cun above the posterior end of the axillary fold, at the lateral margin of the scapula below the infraglenoid tubercle. In the posterior deltoid muscle and in it's deep position in the teres major muscle.

Strikes to this point may cause energy to rush to the head and lead to nausea and even fainting. It may also cause stagnant energy to accumulate at Gb-20, causing headache and confusion.

Activation angle: 90°

SI-10: *Aoshu* (Scapula's Hollow)

When the arm is adducted, the point is directly above SI 9, in the depression inferior and lateral to the scapular spine. In the deltoid muscle posterior to the glenoid fossa of the scapula, and in its deep position, in the infraspinatus muscle.

- Origin Point of the Small Intestine
- Intersection Point of the Yang Linking Vessel
- Intersection Point of the Yang Motility vessel

This strike carries a significant chance of injuring the body physically due to the large number of tendons and muscles located at this point. If the damage is significant enough, knock out may occur as a result of *qi* drainage and pain. Extreme scapular damage may also be experienced.

Activation angle: 45°

SI-11: *Ianzong* (Heaven's Ancestor)

In the infrascapular fossa, at the junction of the upper and middle third of the distance between the lower border of the scapular spine and the inferior angle of the scapula. In the infraspinatus muscle.

This point is capable of immobilizing the entire arm and draining *qi*. Even a medium strike may cause considerable damage to the back and arm.

Immediately, the opponent may feel an "electrical shock" running down their arm; temporary paralysis may then be experienced.

Activation angle: 45°

SI-12: *Bingfeng* (Holding Wind)

Bing means to "receive"; *Feng* means "wind." This point is also translated as "facing" or "controlling wind."

In the center of the suprascapular fossa, directly above SI-11. When the arm is lifted, the point is at the site of the depression.

- Origin Point of the Small Intestine
- Intersection Point of the Gall Bladder
- Intersection Point of the Triple Burner
- Intersection Point of the Large Intestine

When struck hard, this point may cause an energy rush to the head which may effect a knock out. There will likely be a sickly feeling experienced in the upper body for some time afterwards.

The shoulder and scapular region may be dislocated with tendon damage occurring as well.

Activation angle: 45°

SI-13: *Uyuan* (Crooked Wall)

On the medial extremity of the suprascapular fossa, around midway between SI-10 and the 2nd thoracic vertebra spinous process. On the superior margin of the spine of the scapula, in the trapezium and supraspinatus muscles.

This point is considered more dangerous than SI-12 due to the fact that it will drain *qi* rather than increase it.

The lungs can also be physically damaged due to a strike to this point. Scapular damage is also possible from a medium to hard strike.

Activation angle: 45°

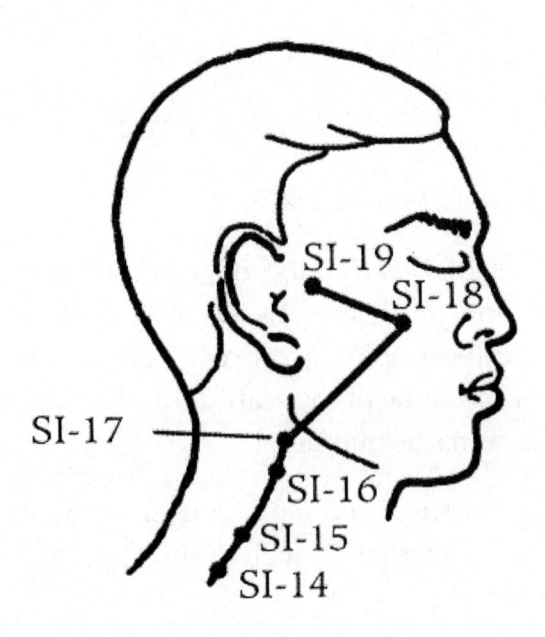

SI-14: *Ianwaishu* (Shoulder's Outer Hollow)

3 cun lateral to the lower border of the spinous process of the 1st thoracic vertebra, on the vertical line drawn upwards from the medial border of the scapula.

Striking this point may shock the upper body and cause the lungs and heart to falter. Extreme nausea may then result with vomiting; death is possible later if left untreated.

Activation angle: 90°

SI-15: *Ianzhongshu* (Mid Shoulder Hollow)

2 cun lateral to the lower border of the spinous process of the 7th cervical vertebra at GV-14. At the end of the transverse process of the 1st thoracic vertebra, superficially in the trapezium and in its deep position, in the levator scapulae muscle.

Striking this point hard may lead to severe *qi* drainage from the upper body leading to nausea and possibly resulting in knock out. Nervous system damage can also occur due to its close proximity to the spinal column.

Activation angle: 90°

SI-16: *Ianchuang* (Heaven's Window)

In the lateral aspect of the neck, on the posterior border of the sternocleidomastoideus muscle, posterior to LI-18, 3.5 cun lateral to the laryngeal prominence.

- Window of the Sky Point
- One of 36 Vital Points Listed in the Bubishi

This is a Window of the Sky point. This point may cause instant death when struck hard. Medium strikes often cause emotional imbalance and heart problems to occur.

Activation angle: 90°

SI-17: *Ianrong* (Heaven's Contents)

Posterior to the angle of the mandible, in the depression on the anterior border of the sternocleidomastoideus muscle and the inferior margin in the posterior belly of the digastric muscle.

- Window of the Sky Point

This point lies very close to the vagus nerve and may cause knock out if struck. It also lies directly over the external carotid artery which will cause a circulation-induced knock out.

This point is also a Window of the Sky point. It is well known for its use in neck locking techniques.

Activation angle: 90°

SI-18: *Uanliao* (Cheek Seam)

Quan means "zygoma" and *liao* means "foramen."

Directly below the outer canthus, in the depression on the lower border of the zygoma, level with LI-20.

- Origin Point of the Small Intestine
- Intersection Point of the Triple Burner

If one uses a small striking surface, such as a single knuckle, a strike may cause knock out since it shocks the brain and may cause a rush of *qi* up the back of the neck to the brain causing confusion.

Activation angle: 45°

SI-19: *Inggong* (Palace of Hearing)

Between the tragus and the mandibular joint, where a depression is formed when the mouth is slightly open. At the anterior of the middle of the tragus, and the posterior margin of the condyle of the mandible.

- Origin Point of the Small Intestine
- Intersection Point of the Gall Bladder

- Intersection Point of the Triple Burner
- Exit Point

The point is well protected by bone and difficult to get at. It is not often used in Martial Arts applications.

Activation angle: 90°

Chapter 5

The Lung Meridian

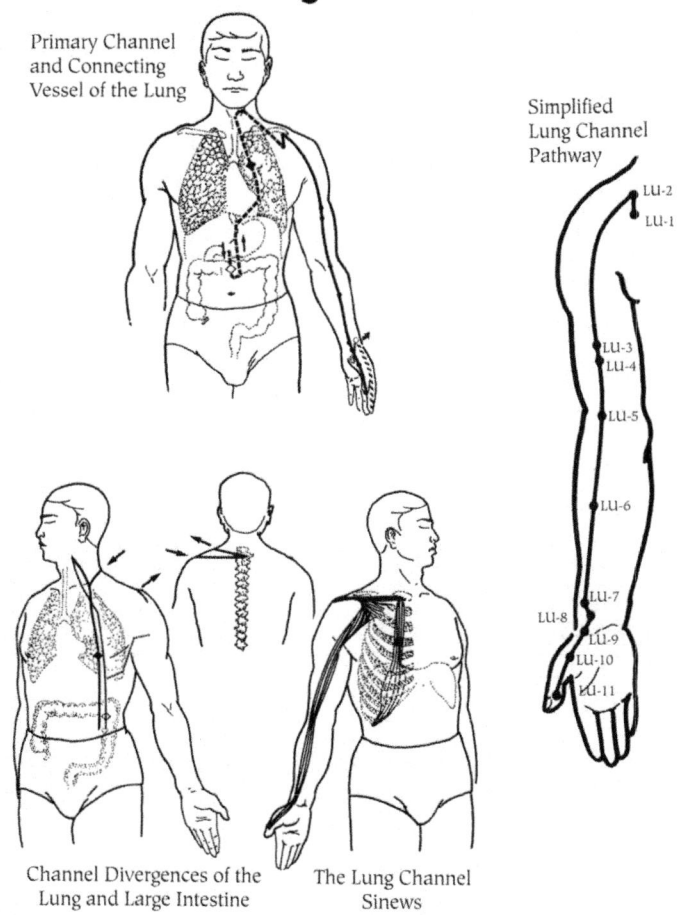

Primary Channel and Connecting Vessel of the Lung

Simplified Lung Channel Pathway

Channel Divergences of the Lung and Large Intestine

The Lung Channel Sinews

Lung Meridian Overview	
Element	Metal
This element creates	Water
This element attacks	Wood
Polarity	Yin / Organ
Coupled Meridian	Large Intestine
Connecting Points	LU-7 & LI-4
Active Time	3:00 to 5:00 am
Entry Point	LU-1
Exit Point	LU-7
Sedation Point	LU-5
Tonification Point	LU-5
Alarm Point	LU-1
Associated Point	BL-13
Source Point	LU-9
Horary Point	LU-8
Wood / Well Point	LU-11
Fire / Spring Point	LU-10
Earth / Stream Point	LU-9
Metal / River Point	LU-8
Water / Sea Point	LU-5

GREATER VESSEL, MAIN CHANNEL:

TENDINO-MUSCULAR MERIDIAN: LU-11 to GB-22 with important gathering points at LU-9, LU-5, and LU-1

DIVERGENT CHANNEL: LU-1, LI-15 to LI-18

LUO LONGITUDINAL CHANNEL:

LUO TRANSVERSE CHANNEL: LU-7 to LI-4 (LI-6 to LU-9)

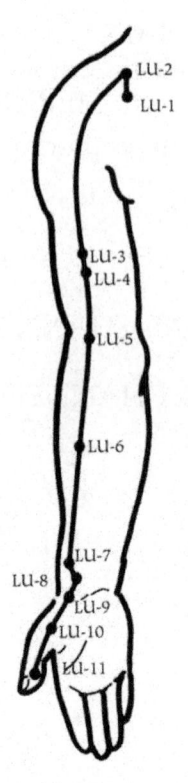

LU-1: *Zhongfu* (Central Residence)

Zhong means "middle" and *fu* means "place." This is referring to the middle *jiao* where the lung channel starts. The *qi* of the spleen and stomach are gathered into the lung at this point. The point is below the acromial extremity of the clavicle, 1 cun directly below LU-2, 6 cun lateral to the CV, in the first intercostal space. In the pectoralis major and minor muscles, in it's deep position, in the internal and external intercostal muscles.

- Intersection Point of the Spleen
- Origin Point of the Lung
- Alarm Point of the Lung
- Entry Point

The lung points all have the possibility of doing great damage. Great *qi* drainage and localized pain may result from strikes.

This point is related to SP-21. A strike may hinder the progress of *gu qi*, or *qi* derived from food and liquid. If this system is impaired, then the body will have a difficult nourishing itself and the recipient's health may decline over time.

Activation angle: 90°

LU-2: *Unmen* (Cloud's Door)

In the depression below the acromial extremity of the clavicle, between the pectoralis major and the deltoid muscles, six cun lateral to the CV channel.

When this point is struck upwards into the clavicle, it is devastating upon the *Qi* of the whole body. The pain can be tremendous. Great internal damage can also be done. This point may cause a knock out or even death through extreme qi drainage.

When the point is struck from the top above the clavicle, the collarbone can be broken.

Activation angle: 90°

LU-3: *Ianfu* (Heaven's Residence)

On the medial aspect of the upper arm, 3 cun below the end of the axillary fold, on the radial side of the biceps brachii, 6 cun above LU-5.

- Window of the Sky Point
- One of 36 Vital Points Listed in the Bubishi

A strike may cause immediate pain to shoot along the entire arm thus paralyzing it temporarily. This is a Window of the Sky point and may imbalance 'heaven and earth,' or head and body causing great emotional problems that will only get worse if left untreated. This strike cause an extreme case of instant vertigo!

Activation angle: 90°

LU-4: *Xiabai* (Gallantry)

Xia means "to press from both sides". *Bai* means "white." When both arms are hanging freely, this point is precisely on both sides of the lungs. On the medial aspect of the upper arm, 1 cun below LU 3, on the radial side of the biceps brachii.

- Destructive Point

This point immediately does the same as LU 3 only the pain and shock can be a little worse. This is also a neurological strike and can disrupt the brain.

Activation angle: 90°

LU-5: *Chize* (Cubit Marsh)

Chi means "ruler or ulna." *Ze* means "marsh." This point is in the depression of the elbow fossa at the ulna aspect. The *Qi* of the channel is infused here, like water flowing into a marsh. On the cubital crease, on the radial side of the tendon of the biceps brachii. The point is located with the elbow slightly flexed. Located in the origin of the brachioradialis muscle.

- Uniting-he Point
- Water Point

- Sedation Point

This point can damage the entire energetic system. It can cause knock out. Strikes can cause the whole upper body to be put out of balance both physically and energetically. A strong strike can also cause brain damage.

Because this point is a 'he' point, it may drain qi from the lungs.

Activation angle: 90°

LU-6: *Ongzui* (Opening Maximum or Supreme Hole)

On the palmar aspect of the forearm, on the line joining LU-9 to LU-5, 7 cun above LU-9. The point is in the brachioradialis muscle, in the lateral margin at the upper extremity of the pronator teres muscle and the medial margin of the extensor carpi radialis brevis and longus muscles.

- Cleft-xi Point

Lower arm paralysis may occur quickly from a hard strike, feeling like a strike to the lungs.

This is a xi-cleft point. It is typically used in an emergency and can release necessary *Qi* to the lungs. This point can be used after striking the attacker in the lung area. When, the body calls for its reserve of *Qi*, it will be unavailable due to the previous strike. This could cause respiratory arrest to result.

Activation angle: 90°

LU-7: *Ieque* (Broken Sequence or Every Deficiency)

Superior to the styloid process of the radius, 1.5 cun above the transverse crease of the wrist, in the depression. When the index fingers and the thumbs of both hands are crossed with the index finger of one hand placed on the styloid process of the radius of the other, the point is in the depression under the tip of the index finger. Between the tendons of the brachioradialis and the abductor pollicis longus muscles.

- Connecting-luo Point of the Large Intestine
- Confluence Point of Conception Vessel
- Frees the channels
- Quickens the Connecting Vessels
- Quickens the Blood
- Command Point of the head and back of neck

- Exit Point

- Master Point of the Conception Vessel

- Coupled Point with Extraordinary Meridian of the Yin Motility Vessel

This point can cause a lot of localized pain and can drain Qi quickly. Even heavy finger pressure here as is the case of a lock, will cause great pain.

A strike here will unbalance the balance of *yin* and *yang* between the lung and large intestine.

Activation angle: 45°

LU-8: *Ingqu* (Across the Ditch)

One cun above the transverse crease of the wrist, in the depression on the radial side of the radial artery. Innervation: The lateral antebrachial cutaneous nerve and the superficial ramus of the radial nerve.

- River-jing Point

- Metal Point

- Horary Point

- One of 36 Vital Points Listed in the Bubishi

This point can cause the *Qi* to drain rapidly. LU-8 used by itself has been known to cause knock out when stimulated too much.

This is a metal, jing, and horary point of the channel and as such when struck will cause the qi to be disrupted in the channel when it is supposed to be active during the 24-hour cycle. This qi imbalance may get worse as each day passes. Sleep will be affected greatly especially between the hours of 3 am and 5 am with the need to urinate because the bladder meridian is at the opposite side of the horary cycle and as such will have the least amount of qi available to it at this time.

Activation angle: 45°

LU-9: *Aiyuan* (Great Abyss or Bigger Deep Hole)

At the transverse crease of the wrist, in the depression on the radial side of the radial artery. At the lateral aspect of the tendon of the flexor carpi radialis muscle and the medial aspect of the tendon of the abductor pollicis longus muscle.

- Source Point
- Stream-shu Point
- Earth Point

- Frees the channels, Quickens the Connecting Vessels
- Meeting-Hui Point of the vessels
- Tonification Point

This is also a great point to drain Qi. It is an earth, source, associated, and a special meeting point of pulse (arteries and veins). It may cause respiration to become erratic causing the recipient to feel suffocated.

Activation angle: 45°

LU-10: *Uji* (Fish Border)

On the radial aspect of the midpoint of the first metacarpal bone, at the junction of the red and white skin (the lighter colored and darker colored skin). In the lateral abductor pollicis brevis and opponens pollicis muscles.

- Spring-ying Point
- Fire Point
- Destructive Point

This is an excellent point to use to help do wrist locks and turns. It causes the opponent's legs to buckle when pressed inward towards the bone.

Activation angle: 45°

LU-11: *Haoshang* (Lessor Merchant)

On the radial side of the thumb, about 0.1 cun posterior to the radial corner of the nail.

- Uniting-He Point
- Well-jing Point
- Wood Point
- Revives consciousness

This is a wood and cheng point and can be used for the healing of muscles and tendons. In healing, it is used to increase the Wei qi to the surface of the skin when external pathogenic attack is imminent. It has little Martial value.

Activation angle: 45°

Chapter 6

The Large Instestine Meridian

Primary Channel and Conncecting Vessel of the Lung

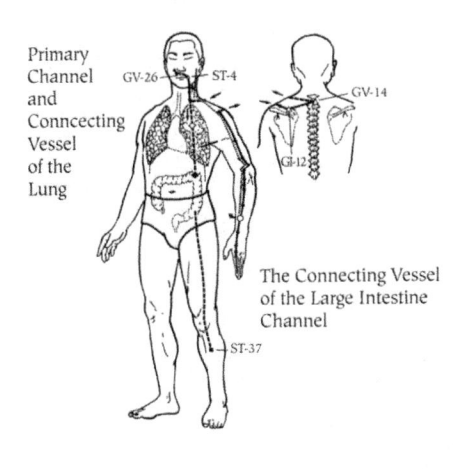

GV-26, ST-4, GV-14, GI-12

The Connecting Vessel of the Large Intestine Channel

ST-37

Channel Divergences of the Large Intestine and Lung

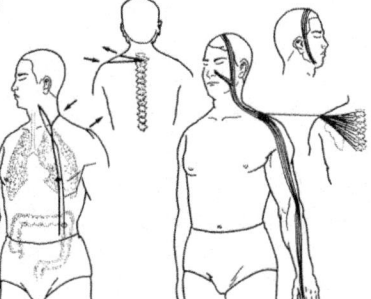

The Large Intestine Channel Sinews

LI-20, LI-19, LI-18, LI-17, LI-16, LI-15, LI-14, LI-13, LI-12, LI-11, LI-10, LI-9, LI-8, LI-7, LI-6, LI-5, LI-4, LI-3, LI-2, LI-1

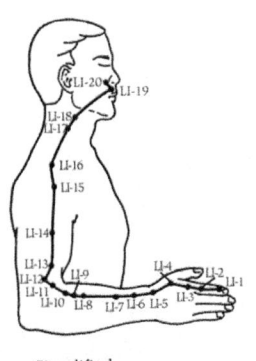

Simplified Large Intestine Channel Pathway

Large Intestine Meridian Overview	
Element	Metal
This element creates	Water
This element attacks	Wood
Polarity	Yang / Bowel
Coupled Meridian	Lung
Connecting Points	LI-6 and LU-9
Active Time	5:00 to 7:00 pm
Entry Point	LI-4
Exit Point	LI-20
Sedation Point	LI-2
Tonification Point	LI-11
Alarm Point	ST-25
Associated Point	BL-25
Source Point	LI-4
Horary Point	LI-1
Metal / Well Point	LI-1
Water / Spring Point	LI-2
Wood / Stream Point	LI-3
Fire / River Point	LI-5
Earth / Sea Point	LI-11
Meridian Connections	GV-14 GV-26 LI-15 (Yang Heel)

GREATER VESSEL: From the radial side of the tip of the index finger, it runs proximally along the radial side of the index finger and passes through the interspace between the first and second metacarpal bones through the anatomical snuff-box and continues along the lateral aspect of the elbow crease. From there it arises along the lateral aspect of the upper arm to the shoulder joint and crosses behind the shoulder to the depression between the scapular spine and the lateral extremity of the clavicle and then travels medially, passing through SI-12 to GV-14. From GV-14 it enters the supraclavicular fossa in the region ST-12 and connects with the Lung before descending through the diaphragm to join with the Large Intestine. Another branch ascends from the supraclavicular fossa along the lateral aspect of the neck, to enter the lower gums where it then exits at ST-4, curves around the upper lip and crosses to the opposite side of the body at GV-26. From GV-26, the left meridian crosses to the right and the right meridian travels to the left to terminate either side of the nose LI.-20. According to the Spiritual Pivot a branch of the Large Intestine primary channel descends to ST-37.

TENDINO MUSCULAR MERIDIAN: LI-1 to GB-13

DIVERGENT CHANNEL (DISTINCT MERIDIAN): LI-15, LU-1 TO LI-18

LONGITUDINAL LUO CHANNEL: LI-6

TRANSVERSE LUO CHANNEL: LI-6 to LU-9

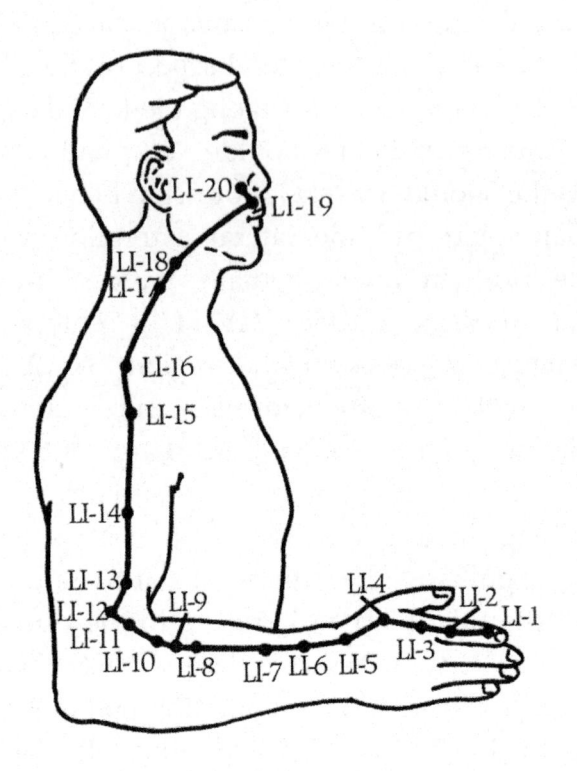

LI-1: *Shangyang* (Shang Yang)
On the radial side of the index finger, about 0.1" proximal to the corner of the nail.

- Well-jing Point
- Metal Point

- Horary Point

This is a metal point and can be used to treat coma.

Activation angle: 15°

LI-2: *Erjian* (Second Space)
On the radial side of the index finger, distal to the metacarpophalangeal joint, at the border of the red and white skin. the point is located with the finger slightly flexed.

- Spring-ying Point
- Water Point
- Sedation Point

This is a Water point. It is often used in conjunction with SI-5. Finger pressure will release the finger.

Activation angle: 90°

LI-3: *Sanjian* (Third Space)
On the radial side of the index finger proximal to the head of the 2nd metacarpal bone. Easily located when a loose fist is formed.

- Wood Point

85

- Stream-shu Point

- Sedation Point

This is a Wood point which can cause localized pain in the hand when manipulated. Finger pressure will release the finger.

Activation angle: 90°

LI-4: *Hegu* (Union Valley)
In the center of the flesh between the 1st and 2nd metacarpal bones, slightly closer to the 2nd metacarpal bone. In the transverse crease of the interphalangeal joint of the thumb of one hand is lined up with the margin of the web between the thumb and the index finger of the other hand, the point is where the tip of the thumb touches.

- Source Point

- Regulates the Spleen and Stomach

- Command Point of the face and mouth

- Entry Point

- One of 36 Vital Points Listed in the Bubishi

This point is an entry and source point. In the healing arts, it is used to relieve headaches. This point causes the body to release endorphins when manipulated, which are pain killers. It has limited use in Martial Arts due to this. If struck straight in, it can cause pain however.

Activation angle: 90°

LI-5: *Yangxi* (Yang Ravine)
On the radial side of the wrist. When the thumb is extended it is in the depression between the tendons of the long and short extensor muscles of the thumb (m. extensor pollicis longus and m. extensor pollicis brevis).

- Fire Point
- River-jing Point
- Destructive Point

This is a Fire point. When manipulated, it can cause localized pain in the hand. It is often used in wrist latches.

Activation angle: 90°

LI-6: *Pianli* (Veering Passage)
One quarter of the way (or 3") along the line that runs from LI-5 to LI-11.

- Connecting-luo Point of the Lung

- Associated with an Extraordinary Vessel

A connecting point. When manipulated, this point can cause massive amounts of energy drainage. It is often employed in wrist latches.

This point is often coupled with LI-17 or LI-18.

Activation angle: 45°

LI-7: *Wenliu* (Warm Flow)
With the ulna facing down and the elbow flexed, this point is 5" above LI-5. Locate the point while making a fist.

- Regulates the Spleen and Stomach
- Cleft-xi Point

This point can cause localized pain in the hand.

Activation angle: 45°

LI-8: *Xialian* (Lower Ridge)
Located 4" below LI-11.

Comparable to LI-7.

Activation angle: 45°

LI-9: *Shanglian* (Upper Ridge)
Located 1" above LI-8 and 3" below LI-11 on the line running from LI-5 to LI-11.

When struck, this point has the ability to quicken the connecting vessel. Physically, it can cause temporary paralysis of the arm.

Activation angle: 45°

LI-10: *Shousanli* (Arm Three Li)
Located 2" below LI-11 on the line drawn from LI-5.

- One of 36 Vital Points Listed in the Bubishi

This point can cause temporary paralysis of the arm. If struck harder, it may cause immediate diarrhea.

Striking this point towards the hand causes the head to come towards you, exposing the neck and head to the next attack. It is often coupled with LI-18 strikes.

Activation angle: 90°

LI-11: *Quchi* (Pool at the Bend)
When the elbow is flexed the point is in the depression at the lateral end of the transverse cubital crease, midway between LU-5 and the lateral epicondyle of the humerus.

- Uniting-He Point
- Earth Point
- Regulates the Spleen and Stomach
- Tonification Point

This is a tonification and earth point. Struck with medium power, it can cause temporary paralysis of the arm. Harder strikes may cause vomiting and diarrhea.

It is comparable in effect to LI-10.

Activation angle: 90°

LI-12: *Zhouliao* (Elbow Bone-hole)
When the elbow is flexed, the point is superior to the epicondyle of the humerus, about 1" superolateral to LI-11.

This is a sedation point. It is known to quicken the connecting vessel.

It has the ability to drain energy from the arm. If struck with more power, it can cause temporary paralysis of the arm.

Activation angle: 45°

LI-13: *Shouwui* (Arm Five Li)
Located 3" above LI-11 on the line joining LI-11 and LI-15.

- Origin Point of the Liver
- Intersection Point of the Yin Linking Vessel
- Frees the Channels
- Quickens the Connecting Vessels

This point is known to quicken the connecting vessel. Medium power strikes may cause temporary paralysis of the arm. Even lighter strikes will cause localized pain.

This is noted by some as a Forbidden Point in acupuncture.

Activation angle: 90°

LI-14: *Binao* (Upper Arm)
On the upper arm, slightly superior to the insertion of the deltoid muscle (m. deltoideus), on the line connecting LI-11 and LI-15.

- Intersection Point of the Bladder
- Intersection Point of the Small Intestine
- Origin Point of the Large Intestine
- Intersection Point of the Yang Linking Vessel

This is the intersection-*jiaohui* point of the hand *Yang ming* large intestine channel with the foot *Yang ming* stomach meridian and the *Yang* linking vessel.

If struck hard, it may cause emotional problems later in life.

Activation angle: 90°

LI-15: *Jianyu* (Shoulder Bone)
Inferior to the acromion, and slightly anterior to the middle of the upper portion of the deltoid muscle (m. deltoideus). When the arm is in full abduction, the point is in the anterior of the two depressions appearing at the border of the acromiohumeral junction.

- Origin Point of the Large Intestine

- Intersection Point of the Yang Motility vessel

This is the intersection-*jiaohui* point of the hand *tai yang* small intestine channel with the hand *yang ming* large intestine channel and the *yang* motility vessel.

Activation angle: 90°

LI-16: *Jugu* (Great Bone)
On the superior aspect of the shoulder, in the depression between acromial extremity of the clavicle and the scapular spine.

- Origin Point of the Large Intestine

- Intersection Point of the Yang Motility vessel

This is the intersection-*jiaohui* point of the hand *yang ming* large intestine channel and the *yang* motility vessel.

When struck, this point can drain energy from the body, but it has limited Martial application.

Activation angle: 90°

LI-17: *Tianding* (Celestial Tripod)
On the anterior lateral aspect of the neck superior to the midpoint of the supraclavicular fossa, on the posterior border of the sternocleidomastoid muscle (m. sternocleidomastoideus).

Striking this point can prove fatal if struck hard enough! It disrupts the energy of the lungs.

LI-18: *Futu* (Protuberance Assistant)
On the lateral aspect of the neck, level with the tip of the adam's apple, between the sternal head and clavicular head of the sternocleidomastoid muscle (m. sternocleido-mastoideus).

- Window of the Sky Point

This is a Window of the Sky point and is responsible for controlling the energy flowing to the head.

A strike is capable of disconnecting the upper and lower bodies from each other and impairing their communication. Strikes are likely to drive energy up into the brain and can easily induce knock out. More powerful strikes can be fatal.

This point is also dangerous due to its location on the cervical artery. If plaque has built up in the individual and the point is struck hard, then there is a possibility of a piece of plaque breaking loose and getting lodged in the small vessels and capillaries in the brain and inducing an aneurism.

Its connection with the occipital nerve easily causes black out when struck.

This point is often used in knock outs, but remember that this is a very dangerous point!

Activation angle: 90°

LI-19: *Heliao* (Grain Bone-hole)
Directly below the lateral margin of the nostril, level with GV-26.

This point is capable of causing localized pain and has a very shocking effect on the body when struck.

Activation angle: 45°

LI-20: *Yingxiang* (Welcome Fragrance)
In the nasolabial groove, at the level of the midpoint of the lateral border of ala nasi.
- Intersection Point of the Stomach
- Origin Point of the Large Intestine

- Exit Point

This is an exit and intersection-jiaohui point of the hand *yang ming* large intestine and foot *yang ming* stomach channels.

This point is often used in knock out techniques.

Activation angle: 45°

Chapter 7

The Liver Meridian

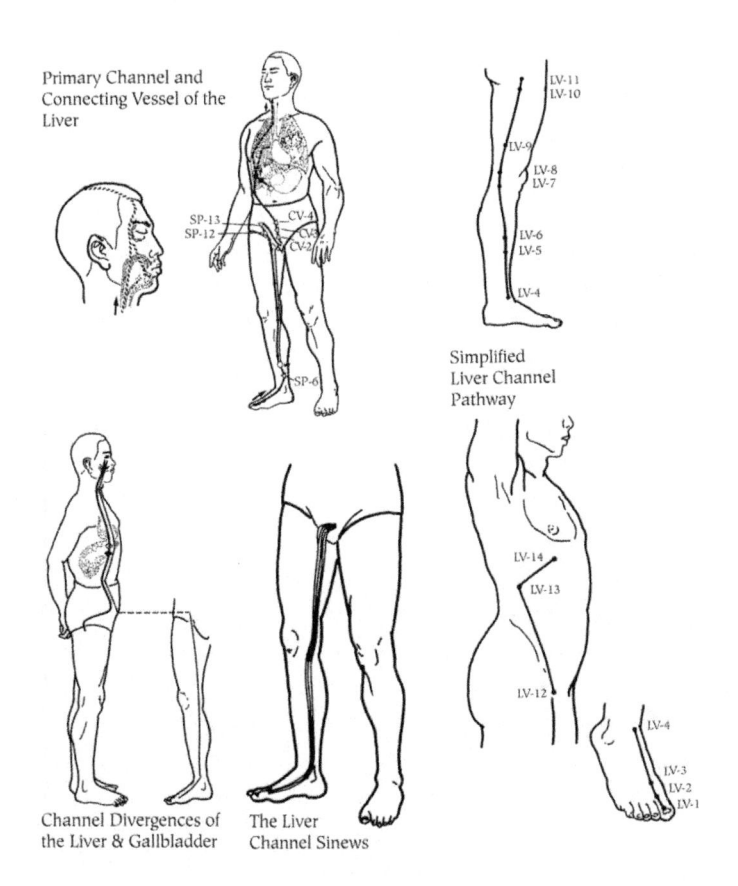

Liver Meridian Overview	
Element	Wood
This element creates	Fire
This element attacks	Earth
Polarity	Yin / Organ
Coupled Meridian	Gall Bladder
Connecting Points	LV-5 & GB-40
Active Time	1:00 to 3:00 am
Entry Point	LV-1
Exit Point	LV-14
Sedation Point	LV-2
Tonification Point	LV-8
Alarm Point	LV-14
Associated Point	BL-18
Source Point	LV-3
Horary Point	LV-1
Wood / Well Point	LV-1
Fire / Spring Point	LV-2
Earth / Stream Point	LV-3
Metal / River Point	LV-4
Water / Sea Point	LV-8
Meridian Connections	CV-2
	CV-3
	CV-4
	LV-13 (Yin Linking)

GENERAL/ELEMENTAL QUALITIES:

The Liver has five primary functions: stores blood, maintains the free flow of the qi, dominates the sinews, opens into the eyes, and manifests in the nails.

In addition the Liver zang belongs to the wood phase and corresponds to wind. The Liver governs uprising, and in disharmony its qi may therefore rise excessively. The Liver is entrusted with the ming men fire which in disharmony may easily flare upwards as pathological heat.

The Liver free-flowing function assists the qi movement of the zangfu, especially the descending of Lung and Stomach qi and the ascending of Spleen qi.

The Liver free-flowing function assists the qi transformation function of the Bladder. Liver stores the ethereal soul (hun) and as the wood zang is the 'mother' of the Heart. Liver stores the blood which flows into the Conception and Thoroughfare Vessel to become menstrual blood, and its qi is responsible for the smooth flow of menstrruation.

GREATER VESSEL:

Starts on the lateral aspect of the dorsum of the big toe and runs along the foot to 1 cun anterior to the medial malleolus, it ascends intersecting the Spleen meridianl SP-6, then continues to ascend anterior to the Spleen channel to an area 8 cun above the medial malleolus, where it crosses and continues posterior to the Spleen channel up to the knee and the medial aspect of the thigh,continues to the pubic region via SP-12 and SP-13 where it encircles the genitals, then ascends to enter the lower abdomen where it intersects the Conception vessel at Qugu CV-2, Zhongji CV-3 and Guanyuan CV-4.

It continues upwards to curve round the Stomach before entering the Liver and connecting with the Gall Bladder, crosses the diaphragm and spreads in the costal and hypochondriac region, ascends along the neck and posterior aspect of the throat to the nasopharynx to link with the tissues surrounding the eye, ascends across the forehead to the vertex where it intersects with the Governing vessel at GV-20. A branch descends from the eye system through the cheek and encircles the inner surface of the lips. Another branch separates from the Liver, crosses the diaphragm and spreads in the Lung, meeting with MH-1

TENDINO MUSCULAR (SINEW) MERIDIAN: Starting at LV-1 it proceeds up to CV-2,3 along the medial aspect of the leg with gathering points at LV-4 and LV-8

DIVERGENT CHANNEL (DISTINCT MERIDIAN): LV-12 (GB-30) up to GB-1

LONGITUDINAL LUO CHANNEL: LV-5 up to the genitals

TRANSVERSE LUO CHANNEL: LV-5 to GB-40

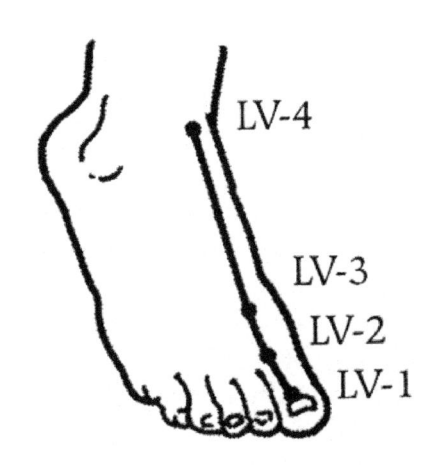

LV-1: *Dadun* (Large Hill) or (Great Honesty)

On the lateral aspect of the dorsum of the big toe, 0.1 cun proximal to the corner of the nail.

- Uniting-He Point
- Well-jing Point
- Wood Point
- Intersection Point of the Bladder
- Horary Point
- Entry Point

This is a "wood and cheng" point. The liver is in charge of transferring *Qi* out to all areas of the body. It also controls the body's defenses.

Used with LV-13, this point may cause great internal damage in addition to energy damage. Death may result when LV-13 is struck hard. LV-1 struck alone may cause nausea.

Activation angle: 90°

LV-2: *Xingjian* (Active Interval) or (Walk Between)

On the web between the big and second toes slightly closer to the big toe.

- Spring-ying Point
- Fire Point

- Quickens the Blood
- Sedation Point

This is a fire and stream point. This point causes fire in the liver. Localized pain and *Qi* drainage are normal.

Activation angle: 90°

LV-3: *Taichong* (Supreme Assault) or (Great Pouring)

On the dorsum of the foot, between the ossa metatarsal 1 and 2 in the depression posterior to the art, metatarso-phalangae. A very sore spot just up from LV-2 between the big and second toes slightly towards the big toe.

- Source Point
- Stream-shu Point
- Earth Point
- Quickens the Blood
- One of 36 Vital Points Listed in the Bubishi

This is an earth, associated, and source point. This point draws from Ancestral *Qi*.

A strike on LV-3 will often immobilize an attacker. The localized pain is great and massive qi drainage may occur.

Activation angle: 90°

LV-4: *Zhongfeng* (Middle Seal)

1 cun anterior to the medial malleous, midway between SP-5 and ST-41, in the depression on the medial side of the tendon of Tibialis anterior. Above the tubercle of the navicular, medial to the anterior Tibialis tendon.

- River-jing Point
- Metal Point
- Quickens the Blood

This point is relatively difficult to strike, but will simulate the effect of a strike to the groin. Localized pain and ankle damage may result.

Activation angle: 45°

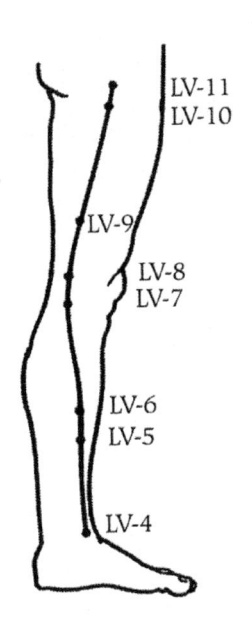

LV-5: *Tioga* (Worm Eater's Groove)

5 cun above the tip of the medial malleolus, on the medial aspect near the medial border of the Tibia. One third of the length from the tip of the malleolus to the mid point of the Knee.

- Connecting-luo Point of the Gall Bladder
- Quickens the Blood

This point may cause nausea when struck, followed by abdominal cramping.

Activation angle: 15°

LV-6: *Zhongfu* (Middle Metropolis)

Seven cun above the medial malleus, or 2 cun above LV-5, on the medial aspect near the border of the Tibia.

- Cleft-xi Point

This is a Xie-cleft point so it is an accumulation point for Qi. Striking this point may cause localized pain and muscle spasms in the legs. It may also cause nausea.

Struck hard, it may force the opponent to the ground without much damage.

Activation angle: 15°

LV-7: *Xiguan* (Knee's Hinge)

Posterior and inferior to the medial Condyle of the Tibia, in the upper portion of the medial head of the Gastrocnemious, I cun posterior to SP-9.

Great localized pain may result when struck. It can be applied with either the foot or by finger pressure during grappling.

Activation angle: 45°

LV-8: *Ququan* ("Crooked Spring")

On the medial side of the Knee joint, when then Knee is flexed, the point is above the medial end of the transverse popliteal crease, posterior to the medial condyle of the Tibia, on the Anterior border of the insertion of Semimbranosus and Semitendinous.

- Uniting-He Point
- Water Point
- Tonification Point

This is a water point. Striking this point will often cause the opposite to occur. It may cause the system to heat.

Nausea may result from a strike. This point may also hinder the circulating of *Qi* in the liver meridian. It may have an immediate effect upon the liver causing it to become hot, thus unbalancing the body.

Activation angle: 90°

LV-9: *Yinbao* (Yin's Wrapping)

4 cun above the medial epicondial of the Femur, between Vastus Medialis and Satorius.

This point is a common knock out point that can be used effectively by most people with little knowledge.

Activation angle: 90°

LV-10: *Zuwuli* (Five Measures of the Foot)

Location 3 cun below ST 30, on the lateral border of Abductor Longus, 1 cun below LV-11.

This point may cause localized pain and massive *Qi* drainage. Struck hard, it may affect the eyes.

Activation angle: 90°

LV-11: *Yinlian* (Yin's Modest)

2 cun below ST-30, on the lateral border of Abductor Longus, On the medial border of the thigh.

- One of 36 Vital Points Listed in the Bubishi

This point may affect the spleen. It may cause the legs and arms to weaken.

Activation angle: 90°

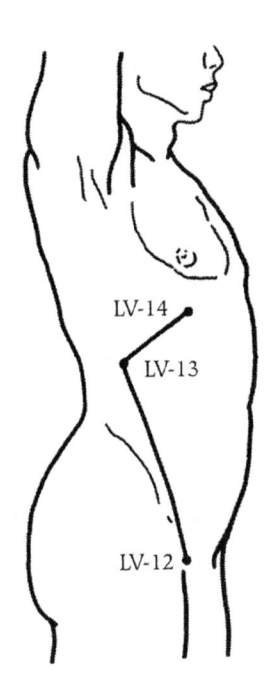

LV-12: *Jimai* (Urgent Pulse)

Inferior and lateral to the pubic symphysis, 2.5 cun lateral to the CV meridian, at the inguinal groove lateral and inferior to ST-30.

Struck hard enough, this point can be lethal. A light to medium strike may cause the genitals to bleed. Internal physical injury may be caused to the tendons and muscles in this area.

This point also has an effect upon the *tantien*, causing the energy flow to the whole body to become erratic. GB-24 is often struck in unison with this point for a devastating effect.

Activation angle: 90°

LV-13: *Zhangmen* (System's Door)

On the lateral side of the abdomen, below the free end of the 11th rib, when the arm is bent at the elbow and held against the side, the point is roughly located at the tip of the elbow. This point is in the internal and external oblique muscles.

- Intersection Point of the Bladder
- Alarm Point of the Spleen
- Quickens the Blood
- Meeting-Hui Point of the viscera
- Associated with an Extraordinary Vessel of the Yin Motility vessel
- One of 36 Vital Points Listed in the Bubishi

Great physical damage can be done when this point is struck. This is one of the more dangerous points on the body.

The spleen is easily ruptured with a strike here.

The liver is also affected by a strike, resulting in liver and spleen damage.

Activation angle: 90°

LV-14: *Qimen* (Expectation's Door)

On the mamillary line, two ribs below the nipple, in the 6th intercostal space. This point is 6 cun above the navel and 3.5 cun lateral to GV-14, near the medial end of the 6th intercostal space in the internal and external oblique muscles and the aponeurosis of the transverse abdominal muscle.

- Intersection Point of the Spleen
- Origin Point of the Liver
- Alarm Point of the Liver
- Exit Point

This point may cause mental problems and heart problems. It can even cause cardiac arrest! It can also cause the lungs to collapse, resulting in respiratory arrest!

The liver may also be made to stop functioning as a result of a hard strike. Even a light strike here will cause damage.

Knock out may occur immediately due to great energy drainage, even stopping the *Qi* temporarily. This point is one of the delayed death touch points.

Activation angle: 45°

Chapter 8

The Gall Bladder Meridian

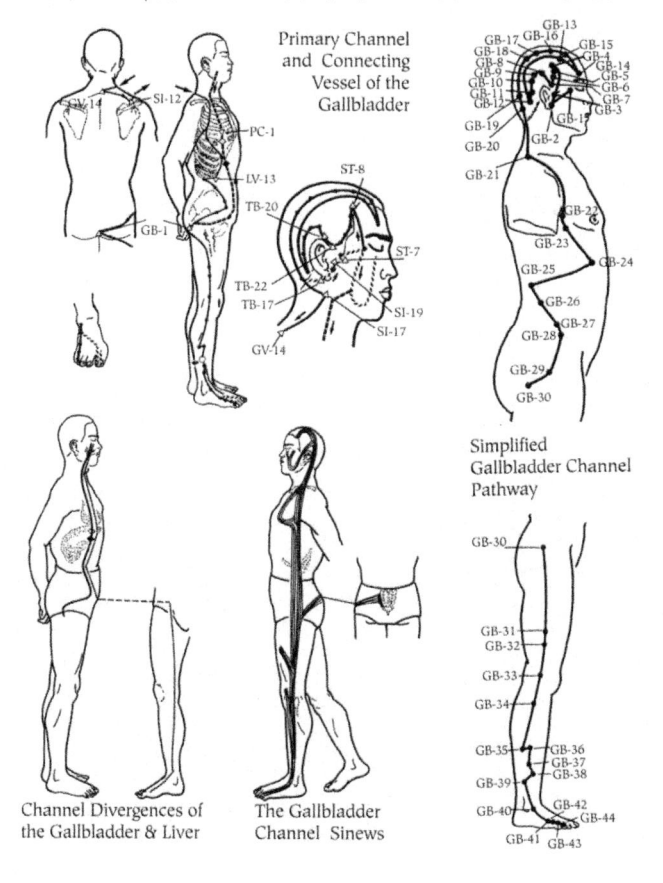

Primary Channel and Connecting Vessel of the Gallbladder

Channel Divergences of the Gallbladder & Liver

The Gallbladder Channel Sinews

Simplified Gallbladder Channel Pathway

Gall Bladder Meridian Overview	
Element	Wood
This element creates	Fire
This element attacks	Earth
Polarity	Yang / Bowel
Coupled Meridian	Liver
Connecting Points	GB-37 & LV-3
Active Time	11:00 pm to 1:00 am
Entry Point	GB-1
Exit Point	GB-41
Sedation Point	GB-38
Tonification Point	GB-43
Alarm Point	GB-24
Associated Point	BL-19
Source Point	GB-40
Horary Point	GB-41
Metal / Well Point	GB-44
Water / Spring Point	GB-43
Wood / Stream Point	GB-41
Fire / River Point	GB-38
Earth / Sea Point	GB-34

GREATER VESSEL:

The Gall Bladder meridian starts at the outer canthus of the eye. It ascends the forehead and curves downwards to the region behind the ear (at Fengchi GB-20). From here it runs down the neck to the supraclavicular fossa.

A branch from the region behind the ear enters the ear. Another branch from the outer canthus meets the Triple Burner channel in the infer orbital region. It then descends to the neck and the supraclavicular fossa where it meets the main branch. From here, it descends to the chest and passing through the diaphragm, it enters the liver and gall bladder. It then runs down the hypochonriac region and the later al side of the abdomen to reach the point Huantiao GB-30.

The main portion of the channel from the supraclivcualar fossa goes to the axilla and the lateral side fo the chest to the ribs and hip where tit meets the previous branch. It then descends along the lateral aspect of the thigh and leg to end at the lateral side of the 4th toe.

From Zulinqi GB-41, a branch goes to Dan LV-1.

TENDINO MUSCULAR MERIDIAN: GB-45 TO SI-18

DIVERGENT CHANNEL (DISTINCT MERIDIAN): GB-30, LV-12 to GB-1

LONGITUDINAL LUO CHANNEL: GB-37

TRANSVERSE LUO CHANNEL: GB-37 to LV-3

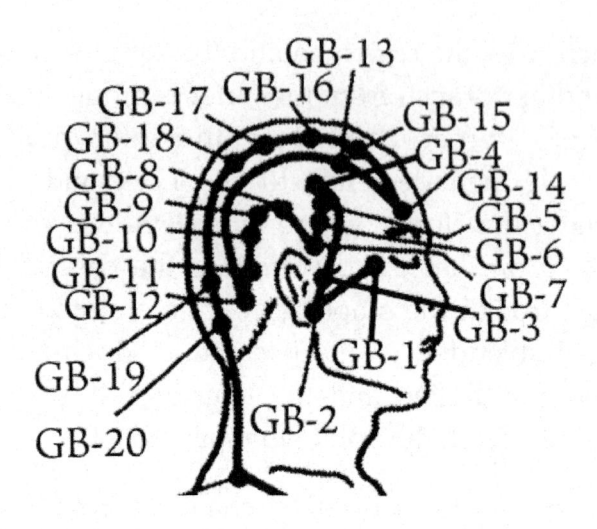

GB-1: *Tonqziliao* (Bone Of The Eye)

.5 cun lateral to the outer edge of the canthus of the eye. The point is in the orbicularis muscle. The nerves in the region include the zygomaticofacial, zygomaticotemporal and the temporal and frontal branches or the facial nerve.

- Intersection Point of the Small Intestine

- Origin Point of the Gall Bladder
- Intersection Point of the Triple Burner
- Entry Point

Struck alone, this point may cause extreme nausea, loss of memory, and even possible death. It is very dangerous, even when struck lightly. The eyes may also be damaged from a strike.

Activation angle: 15°

GB-2: *Tinghui* (Confluence of Hearing)

In front of the intertragic notch, directly below "Tinggong" at the posterior border of the condyloid process of the mandible. Locate the point with the mouth open.

Struck alone, this point may also cause extreme nausea and dizziness. The point may be lethal if struck hard.

Activation angle: 15°

GB-3: *Shangquan* (Guests & Hosts)

This is the temple point. On the superior border of the zygomatic arch, in the depression which can be felt in the bone. The zygomatic branch of the facial nerve and the zygomaticofacial nerve, the zygomaticoorbital artery and vein.

- Origin Point of the Gall Bladder
- Intersection Point of the Triple Burner
- Intersection Point of the Stomach
- One of 36 Vital Points Listed in the Bubishi

This point may cause death when struck hard and knock out when struck lightly or with medium power.

Activation angle: 15°

GB-4: *Han Yan* (Satisfying Jaw)

Within the hairline of the temporal region, ¼ of the distance from ST-8 to GB-7. Or one cun below ST-8. Movement can be felt at this point when chewing.

- Origin Point of the Gall Bladder
- Intersection Point of the Triple Burner
- Intersection Point of the Stomach

This point may cause death when struck hard. A light blow may cause dizziness.

Activation angle: 15°

GB-5: *Xuanlu*: (Suspended Head)

In the middle of the curve between ST-8 and GB-7.

- Origin Point of the Gall Bladder
- Intersection Point of the Triple Burner
- Intersection Point of the Stomach
- Intersection Point of the Large Intestine

This point is very comparable to GB-4. If GB-4, 5, 6 and 7 are struck simultaneously, the result is more detrimental.

Activation angle: 15°

GB-6: *Xuanli* (Suspended Balance)

On the hairline between GB-5 and GB-7.

- Origin Point of the Gall Bladder
- Intersection Point of the Triple Burner

- Intersection Point of the Stomach

An artery here may rupture when struck and cause cerebral edema, or brain swelling.

Activation angle: 15°

GB-7: *Qubin* (Crook Of The Temple)

On the hairline in front of the ear apex, one finger width anterior to TH 20.

- Intersection Point of the Bladder
- Origin Point of the Gall Bladder

This point is associated with the small intestine and heart. This point is located near the base of the brain.

Activation angle: 15°

GB-8: *Shuaigu* (Leading To Valley)

Superior to the apex of the auricle, 1.5 cun within the hairline. Or, 1.5 cun above TB-20 which is on the head where the ear apex would touch if pressed inwards.

- Intersection Point of the Bladder

- Origin Point of the Gall Bladder

Knock out may occur with relatively low power strikes.

Death may occur when struck really hard. This point is also a delayed death strike being in close proximity to the small artery on the head.

Activation angle: 15°

GB-9: *Tianchong* (Heavenly Assault)

.5 cun posterior to GB 8, 2 cun within the hairline.

- Intersection Point of the Bladder
- Origin Point of the Gall Bladder

Instant knock out may occur if struck sufficiently hard. Death may occur if struck harder. This point drains energy.

Activation angle: 15°

GB-10: *Fubai* (Floating White)

Posterior and superior to the mastoid process, in the middle of the curved line drawn from GB-9 to GB-11. Or an easier way to find it is on a horizontal line drawn at the level of the eyes that runs towards the back of the head. The point is behind the ear on the squamosal suture which is the joint between the parietal bone and the temporal bone of the skull.

- Intersection Point of the Bladder
- Origin Point of the Gall Bladder

This point affects the brain and the nervous system, impairing motor function. Struck hard enough, it may cause death or knock out.

Activation angle: 15°

GB-11: *Qiaoyin* (Cavity Of Yin)

Midpoint on a line connecting GB-10 and GB-12. It is found in a small hollow behind the ear.

- Intersection Point of the Bladder
- Origin Point of the Gall Bladder

Comparable to the GB-10 point.

Activation angle: 15°

GB-12: *Wangu* (Finished Bone)

In the depression posterior and inferior to the mastoid process, 0.7 cun below GB-11 and level with GV-16.

- Intersection Point of the Bladder
- Origin Point of the Gall Bladder

Death or knock out may occur. This point drains the upper body. It is very dangerous when struck upward.

Activation angle: 15°

GB-13: *Benshen* (Head Above The Tears)

.5 cun inside the hairline and .5 cun medial to ST-8, directly above the outer canthus of the eye. If you drew a line along GB-4, 5, 6, 7 and then went another inch up towards the head, this is close to GB-13.

- Origin Point of the Gall Bladder

This point is located near GB-14 and GB-15 and a strike often hits all three, disrupting the *Qi*.

Activation angle: 15°

GB-14: *Yangbai* (Yang White)

1 cun above the middle of the eyebrow on a line directly above the pupil of the eye in the depression on the superciliary arch.

- Intersection Point of the Small Intestine
- Origin Point of the Gall Bladder
- Intersection Point of the Large Intestine

Struck perpendicular, neck injury may occur. Struck in an upwards fashion can cause energy to rise into the head. Knockout may result when struck downwards draining energy from the head.

Activation angle: 15°

GB-15: *Lingi* (Base Of God)

.5 cun inside the hairline and directly above the pupil when looking ahead.

- Intersection Point of the Bladder
- Origin Point of the Gall Bladder
- Intersection Point of the Yang Linking Vessel

Can cause knock out if struck hard.

Activation angle: 15°

GB-16: *Muchuang* (Window Of The Eyes)

1 cun posterior to GB-15 in straight line with GB-14 and 15.

- Origin Point of the Gall Bladder
- Intersection Point of the Yang Linking Vessel

Localized pain may be experienced from a strike. This point lies along a cranial suture. This point is also located just above the hypothalamus. Strikes to this area may affect the reflexes and coordination.

Activation angle: 15°

GB-17: *Zhengyin* (Principle Yin)

Keep going backwards in a line parallel with the skull 1 cun back from GB-15.

- Origin Point of the Gall Bladder
- Intersection Point of the Yang Linking Vessel

Comparable to GB-16. Knock out and even death may occur from a hard strike.

Activation angle: 15°

GB-18: *Chengling* (Support The Spirit)

1.5 cun posterior to GB-17 on the line connecting GB-15 and GB-20. Approximately 5 cun posterior to the hairline of the forehead. Or approximately 1 cun posterior and 1.2 cun lateral to GV-20.

- Origin Point of the Gall Bladder
- Intersection Point of the Yang Linking Vessel

Light blow may cause knock out. Strikes to this point may scatter the *Qi* of the upper body and affect the *tan tien*.

Hard strikes may impair brain function and even prove fatal.

Activation angle: 15°

GB-19: *Naokong* (Brain Cavity)

Directly above GB-20 level with GV-17 on the lateral side of the external occipital protuberance.

Or, look at the back of the head just above the neck. The bit that sticks out the most is GB-19.

- Origin Point of the Gall Bladder
- Intersection Point of the Yang Linking Vessel

This point is easy to use for a knock out and does not require a lot of power or additional points to make it work.

Activation angle: 15°

GB-20: *Fengchi* (Pool Of Wind)

In the posterior aspect of the neck, below the occipital bone, in the depression between the upper portion of the sternocleidomastoideus muscle and the Trapezius muscle.

- Origin Point of the Gall Bladder
- Intersection Point of the Yang Linking Vessel
- Intersection Point of the Yang Motility vessel
- Lowers the blood pressure

Very common knock out point! Strikes made in an upward direction may cause a knockout. Hard strikes may injure the brain and cause death.

Activation angle: 45°

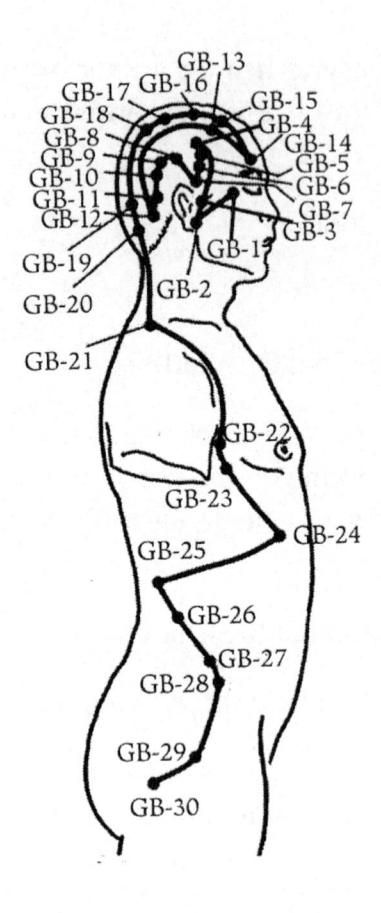

GB-21: *Jianjing* (Shoulder Well)

Midway between GV-14 and the acromion of the shoulder, at the highest point of the shoulder.

- Origin Point of the Gall Bladder
- Intersection Point of the Triple Burner
- Intersection Point of the Stomach
- Intersection Point of the Yang Linking Vessel

This point drains qi (energy) from the head and may cause knock out if struck hard enough.

This point is also a neurological shut down point.

Activation angle: 90°

GB 22: *Yuanye* (Gulf's Fluids)

On the mid-axillary line, 3 cun below the axilla and in the 5th intercostal space.

This point is located near the lymph nodes. It can drain a lot of *Qi*. If death is not instantaneous after a hard strike, it may occur some time later. This point may cause the heart to fail.

Activation angle: 45°

GB-23: *Zhejin* (Flanks Sinews)

1 cun anterior to GB-22, approximately level with the nipple on a male in the 4th intercostal space.

This point drains energy from the body when struck hard.

Activation angle: 45°

GB-24: *Riyue* (Sun Moon)

Inferior to the nipple, between the cartilage of the 7th and 8th ribs, one rib below LV-14.

- Intersection Point of the Bladder
- Origin Point of the Gall Bladder
- Alarm Point of the Gall Bladder
- Quickens the Blood
- One of 36 Vital Points Listed in the Bubishi

Medium power may cause knock out or even death.

Activation angle: 90°

GB-25: *Jingmen* (Door Of The Capital)

Located on the lateral sides of the abdomen, on the lower border of the free end of the twelfth rib.

- Alarm Point of the Kidney

This is the alarm point for the kidneys and can cause great kidney damage when struck from the side. If struck hard, death may result from kidney failure. Light to moderate strikes may cause bleeding from the genitals and great pain in the kidney region.

Activation angle: 45°

GB-26: *Daimai* (Girdle Vessel)

Directly below the free end of the eleventh rib, where LV-13 is located, level with the umbilicus. The point lies in the external oblique muscle and the internal oblique and transverse abdominal muscles.

- Origin Point of the Gall Bladder
- Intersection Point of the Girdling Vessel

This point may cause pain in the gall bladder area. If struck hard enough, death may result from heart failure.

Activation angle: 90°

GB-27: *Wushu* (Five Pivots)

In the lateral sides of the abdomen, in front of the anterior super iliac spine, 3 cun below the level of the umbilicus approximately level with CV-4. In the external &internal oblique muscles and the transverse abdominal muscle.

- Origin Point of the Gall Bladder
- Intersection Point of the Girdling Vessel

Knock out or damage to the kidneys. Hospitalization if strike is hard.

Activation angle: 90°

GB-28: *Weidao* (Meeting Path)

Anterior and inferior to the anterior Iliac spine.

- Origin Point of the Gall Bladder
- Intersection Point of the Girdling Vessel

This point may rupture the bladder when struck hard.

Activation angle: 90°

GB-29: *Juliao* (Bone of Lodging)

Midway between the Anterosuperior iliac spine and the great Trochanter. Locate the point with the person lying on their side. At the anterior margin of the tensor facia lata, and in its deep position in the Vaqstus lateralis muscle.

This point may cause knockout. When combined with strike to GB-12, spasm in the whole upper body may occur.

Activation angle: 90°

GB-30: *Huantiao* (Jumping Circle)

At the junction of the midral thirds of the distance between the Great Trochanter & the Hiatus of the Sacrum (GV-2). When locating this point the person is on their side with their leg flexed. The point is in the Gluteus Maximus and inferior margin of the Piriformus muscle.

- Intersection Point of the Bladder

- Origin Point of the Gall Bladder

- Quickens the Blood

This point may cause knock out and injure the leg. Nausea may result and perhaps bladder problems.

Activation angle: 90°

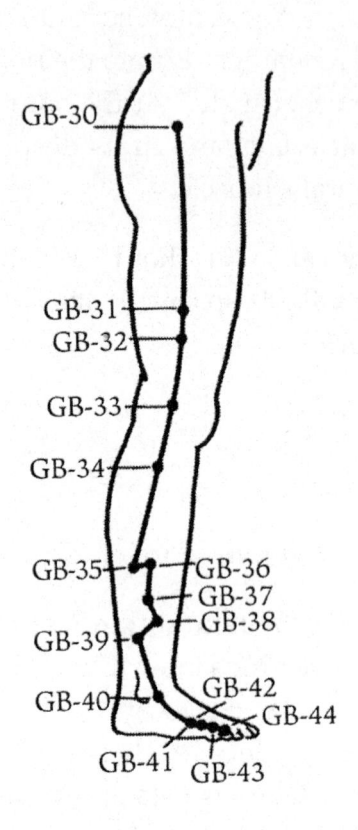

GB-31: *Fenghsi* (City of Wind)

In the mid-line of the lateral aspect of the thigh, 7 cun above the transverse popliteal crease When the patient is standing erect with hands by their sides, the point is located where the tip of the middle finger touches the leg. Beneath the Tensor faciae latae, in the vastus lateralus muscle.

- Quickens the Blood
- One of 36 Vital Points Listed in the Bubishi

This point causes temporary paralysis of the leg. It may also affect the heart. It is easily struck with a knee strike.

Activation angle: 90°

GB-32: *Femur Zhong* (Middle Ditch)

In the lateral aspect of the thigh, 5 cun above the transverse popliteal crease, between the muscle vastus laterals. 2 cun below GB-31.

May cause knockout and injury to the knee. Nausea may result and the heart may be affected.

Activation angle: 90°

GB-33: *Xiyangguan* (Ying Hinge/Gate)

When the knee is flexed, the point is 3 cun above GB 34, lateral to the knee joint in the depression between the tendons of muscles Biceps Femoris and the Femur. In the hollow above the lateral condyle of the femur, at the posterior aspect of the Iliotibial band and the anterior aspect of biceps femoris tendon.

Knock out may occur along with great tendon damage around the knee. This strike will also drain *Qi* quickly.

Activation angle: 90°

GB-34: *Yanglingguan* (Fountain Of The Yang Mound)

In the depression anterior and inferior to the head of the fibula when the leg is flexed. Anterior to the capitulum of the fibula. between peroneus, longis and extensor digitorum longus pedis muscle.

- Lower Uniting-He Point of the Gall Bladder
- Earth Point
- Uniting-He Point of the Gall Bladder
- Quickens the Blood

- Lowers the blood pressure
- Meeting-Hui Point of the sinews

This point can attack the liver. Knockout is likely as well as injury to the leg.

Activation angle: 90°

GB-35: *Yangjiao* (Yang's Intersection)

Seven cun above the lateral malleolus, on the poster border of the fibula, within the distance between the tip of the lateral malleolus and GB-34, level with GB-36 and BL-58. In the lateral aspect of the leg, the distance between the tip of the lateral malleolus and the mid point of the knee is seen as 16 cun.

- Origin Point of the Gall Bladder
- Intersection Point of the Yang Linking Vessel
- Cleft-xi Point

Knock out is possible. This s a Xie-cleft point.

Localized pain is heavy which can cause the nervous system problems. This point may thus be used as a neurological shutdown point.

Activation angle: 90°

GB-36: *Waiqiu* (Outer Mould/External Region)

Seven cun above the lateral malleolus, on the anterior border of the fibular, or midway between GB-34 and the lateral malleolus, in front of GB-35 and level to it at the anterior border of the fibula.

- Cleft-xi Point

This is also a Xie-cleft point comparable to GB-35.

Activation angle: 90°

GB-37: *Guangming* (Bright Light)

Five cun directly above the tip of the external malleus, at the anterior border of the fibula. Between the extensor digitorum longus pedis and peroneus brevis muscles.

- Cleft-xi Point

Localized injury to the shin. The liver and gall bladder may also be damaged.

Activation angle: 90°

GB-38: *Yangfu* (Yang's Help)

Four cun above and slightly anterior to the tip of the External malleolus, on the anterior border of the fibula & the tendons of peroneus longus & brevis.

- Fire Point
- River-jing Point
- Sedation Point

Knock out may result when struck in the proper direction. A hard strike may splinter the shin.

Activation angle: 90°

GB-39: *Xuanzhang* or *Juegu* (Suspended Bell)

3 cun above the tip of the Lateral malleus. In the depression between the posterior border of the fibula and the tendons of peroneus lonaus and brevis. Just above the ankle on the outside of the leg. This is the last GB point above the ankle.

- Meeting-hui Point of the Marrow

A strike may cause energy to be drained from the whole leg area instantly. A few minutes later and the whole body may be drained causing knock out or death.

Activation angle: 90°

GB-40: *Qiuxu*: (Mound of Ruins or Grave Mould) Or (Region Of The Eminence)

Anterior and inferior to the lateral malleolus, in the depression on the lateral side of the tendon of extensor digitorm longus. At the origin of extensor digitorum brevis pedis. Side of the foot, forward of the ankle bone.

- Source Point
- Quickens the Blood

Paralysis may occur if struck very hard. Heart failure and knock out may occur if struck hard.

Activation angle: 90°

GB-41: *Zulinqi* or *Linqi* (Near tears on the foot) or (Lying Down To Weep)

In the depression distal to the junction of the 4th and 5th metatarsal bones, on the lateral side of the tendon of extensor digiti minimi of the foot. About 2 inches back in a straight line from the little toe.

- Wood Point
- Stream-shu Point
- Confluence Point of Girdling Vessel
- Horary Point
- Exit Point
- Master Point of the Girdling Vessel
- Coupled Point with Extraordinary Meridian of the Yang Linking Vessel

This point is a master point for the girdle meridian which runs around the waist. A strike here, not only produces great local pain or a knock out, it may also cause miscommunication between the torso and legs.

Activation angle: 90°

GB-42: *Diwuhui* (Five Terrestrial Reunions) (Earth's Fifth Meeting)

0.5 cun anterior to GB-41, found in the space between the 4th and 5th metatarsal.

This point is comparable to GB-41.

Activation angle: 90°

GB-43: *Xiaxi* (Harmonious River)

0.5 cun behind the margin of the web of the 4th and 5th toes. On the crevice between the 4th and 5th toes.

- Spring-ying Point
- Water Point
- Tonification Point

This is a water and stream or spring point. It can be used to cause dizziness and disorientation and even knock out.

Activation angle: 90°

GB-44: *Qiaoyin* (Yin Cavity)

Lateral side of the tip of the 4th toe. 0.1 cun proximal to the corner of the nail.

- Well-jing Point
- Metal Point

- Destructive Point

This is a metal and well point. It affects the muscles and tendons. A strike here has great physical damage to these areas. It can cause knock out if struck hard enough.

This point is also connected with the liver and may cause extreme nausea.

Activation angle: 15°

Chapter 9

The Spleen Meridian

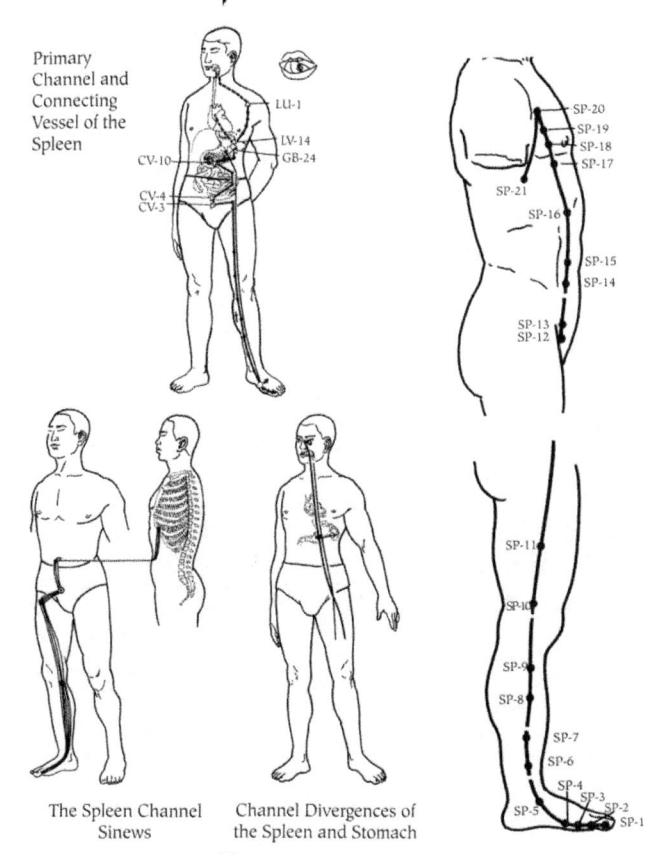

Spleen Meridian Overview	
Element	Earth
This element creates	Metal
This element attacks	Water
Polarity	Yin / Organ
Coupled Meridian	Stomach
Connecting Points	SP-4 & ST-42
Active Time	9:00 to 11:00 am
Entry Point	SP-1
Exit Point	SP-21
Sedation Point	SP-5
Tonification Point	SP-2
Alarm Point	LV-13
Associated Point	BL-20
Source Point	SP-3
Horary Point	SP-3
Wood / Well Point	SP-1
Fire / Spring Point	SP-2
Earth / Stream Point	SP-3
Metal / River Point	SP-5
Water / Sea Point	SP-9

GREATER VESSEL: The spleen channel starts from the tip of the big toe and runs along the medial aspect of the foot to ascend the medial malleolus. It then follows the posterior aspect of the tibia, passes the knee and thigh to enter the abdomen. It then enters the spleen and stomach from where it ascends traversing the diaphragm and reaching the oesophagus. It ends at the center of the tongue. From the stomach, a branch goes through the diaphragm and links with the heart.

TENDINO MUSCULAR MERIDIAN:

DIVERGENT CHANNEL (DISTINCT MERIDIAN): SP-12, ST-30, to BL-1 (ST-1)

LONGITUDINAL LUO CHANNEL:

TRANSVERSE LUO CHANNEL: SP-4 to ST 41

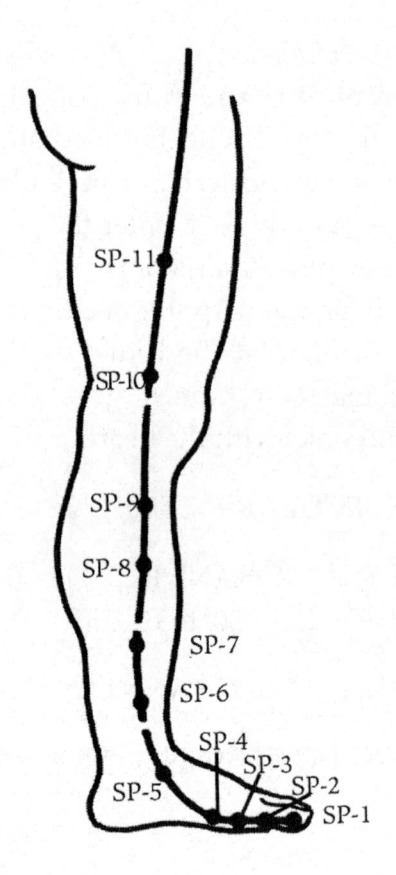

SP-1: *Yinbai* (Hidden White)

On the medial side of the big toe, about 0.1 cun posterior to the corner of the nail.

This is a wood, cheng, and root point of 'Tai Yin" (the greater yin division of Spleen and Lung). This point will affect both the spleen and the lungs since it is the root of the tai yin. It will drain both meridians when struck.

- Uniting-He Point
- Well-jing Point
- Wood Point
- Regulates the Spleen and Stomach
- Entry Point
- Destructive Point

This point is a control point for the muscles, tendons, and divergent meridians. As such, a strike will affect these.

From a healing standpoint, this point may control bleeding in the gastrointestinal tract. When struck, existing bleeding would likely be worsened.

A strike will also impair the communication between the upper and lower halves of the body. A strike can mimic the effects of shock.

Activation angle: 45°

SP-2: *Adu* (Big Metropolis)

On the medial side of the big toe, distal and inferior to the 1st metatarsodigital joint, at the junction of the red and white skin.

- Spring-ying Point
- Fire Point
- Frees the channels, Quickens the Connecting Vessels
- Regulates the Spleen and Stomach
- Tonification Point

This point may be used in grappling techniques to force the opponent to release their hold.

This is a fire and yong point. This point may damage the spleen and weaken it, producing nausea and vomiting. This point may slow the flow of *Qi* in the meridian.

A strike may impair the communication between the upper and lower halves of the body, or heaven and earth.

This point is forbidden during pregnancy.

Activation angle: 45°

SP-3: *Aibai* (Most White)

Proximal and inferior to the head of the 1st metatarsal bone, at the junction of the red and white skin.

- Source Point
- Stream-shu Point
- Earth Point
- Frees the channels
- Quickens the Connecting Vessels
- Regulates the Spleen and Stomach
- Horary Point

This point may cause Qi to drain from the upper chest all the way down to the foot.

Grabbing this point will cause a lot of pain if you can access the point.

This point is an earth, source, and shu point. When struck, this point may cause muscle spasms and cramps. The shock generated can also cause knock out.

Activation angle: 45°

SP-4: *Ongsun* (Grandfather's Grandson)

In the depression distal and inferior to the base of the 1st metatarsal bone, at the junction of the red and white skin or roughly 1 cun behind the joint of the big toe. At the anterior, inferior margin of the 1st metatarsal, in the abductor hallucis muscle.

- Connecting-luo Point of the Stomach
- Confluence Point of Penetrating Vessel
- Frees the channels
- Quickens the Connecting Vessels
- Regulates the Spleen and Stomach
- Master Point of the Penetrating Vessel
- Coupled Point with Extraordinary Meridian of the Yin Linking Vessel

This is a connecting point and a master point for the penetrating vessel. Because of this, a strike may weaken the energy of the body on a permanent basis. Striking this point may impair the uniting of pre and post-natal energy.

A strike may cause intense localized pain and energy drainage. A knock out may also result. Resulting pain may persist for several days.

Striking this point will damage all of the organs and the heart in particular.

Activation angle: 45°

SP-5: *Hangqiu* (Mound of Commerce or Merchant Mould)

In the depression distal and inferior to the medial malleolus, midway between the tuberosity of the navicular bone and the tip of the medial malleolus.

- River-jing Point
- Metal Point
- Regulates the Spleen and Stomach
- Sedation Point

This is a metal and jing point and is related to the joints such as SP-19.

Striking this point causes localized pain and drains energy from the body and will release the joints.

Activation angle: 45°

SP-6: *Anyinjiao* (Three Yin Junction)

Located 3 cun directly above the tip of the medial malleolus, and the posterior border of the tibia, on the line drawn from the medial malleolus to SP-9. Between the posterior max-gin of the tibia and the soleus muscle, and in its deep position in the flexor digitorum longus pedis muscle.

- Origin Point of the Spleen
- Intersection Point of the Liver
- Intersection Point of the Kidney
- Frees the channels
- Quickens the Connecting Vessels
- Regulates the Spleen and Stomach

This is the meeting point of the lower yin meridians. It is often referred to as Inner Gate.

Strikes here may cause great localized pain and nausea.

Activation angle: 45°

SP-7: *Ougu* (Sleeping valley)

6 cun above the tip of the medial malleolus, 3cun above SP 6, at the posterior margin of the tibia.

Can cause intense immediate pain and energy drainage.

Activation angle: 90°

SP-8: *Iji* (Earth's Mechanism)

3 cun below the medial condyle of the tibia, on the line connecting SP-9, and the medial malleolus, between the posterior margin of the tibia and the soleus muscle.

- Frees the channels
- Quickens the Connecting Vessels
- Regulates the Spleen and Stomach
- Cleft-xi Point

This is a xi cleft point, or accumulation point for Zhen Qi, or meridian qi (also known as real qi).

When struck it may cause an obstruction in the meridian and thus spleen problems such as stomach disorders and bladder problems. It may also numb the lower leg.

Activation angle: 90°

SP-9: *Inlingquan* (Yin Tomb Spring or Yin Mould Spring)

On the lower border of the medial condyle of the tibia, in the depression between the posterior border of the tibia and the gastrocnemius in the upper part of the origin of the soleus muscle.

- Uniting-He Point
- Water Point
- Frees the channels
- Quickens the Connecting Vessels
- Regulates the Spleen and Stomach

This is a water and he-sea point.

This point can be lethal due to the fact that it will cause water to accumulate within the body. A hard strike can cause nausea and is sometimes used in connection with GB-34.

Activation angle: 90°

SP-10: *Uehai* (Sea of Blood)

When the knee is flexed, the point is located 2 cun above the mediosuperior border of the patella, on the bulge of the medial portion of the quadriceps femoris, at the superior margin of the medial condyle of the femur, in the medial margin of the vastus medialis muscle. Another way of locating this point is to cup your right palm to the patient's left knee, with the thumb on the medial side and the other four fingers directed proximally, the point is located where the tip of your thumb rests.

- Frees the channels
- Quickens the Connecting Vessels

This point is known to cause shock within the system. This point can cause a lot of pain with low pressure levels alone. With its connection with the blood, it can promote bleeding when struck.

Activation angle: 90°

SP-11: *Imen* (Basket's Door)

6 cun above SP-10, at the medial aspect of the sartorius muscle on the line drawn between SP-10 and SP-12.

This point can affect the transportation of qi via the spleen. This point is often used in conjunction with CV-17.

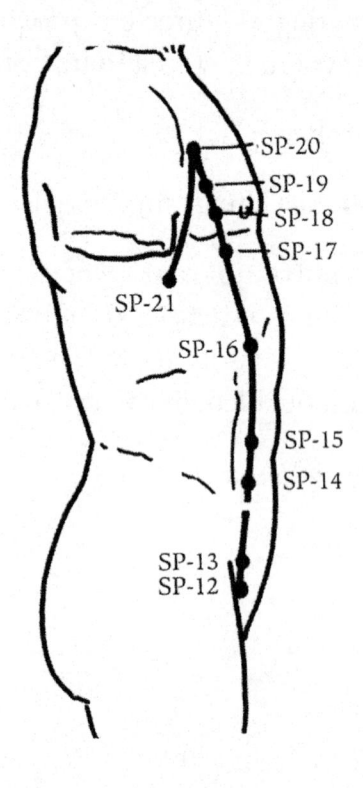

Activation angle: 90°

SP-12: *Hongmen* (Pouring Door)

Superior to the lateral end of the inguinal groove, on the lateral side of the femoral artery, at the level of the upper border of the symphysis pubis, 3.5 cun lateral to CV-2.

- Origin Point of the Spleen
- Intersection Point of the Liver

This point lies directly above the femoral artery and can cause great internal damage to it. It also lies near the femoral nerve and can thus paralyze the whole leg.

A strong strike, such as a kick, to this point can also knock the head of the femur and ball joint rout of its socket damaging the tendons and ligaments leading to great pain and immobilization.

Activation angle: 45°

SP-13: *Ushe* (Dwelling)

0.7 cun above SP 12, 4 cun lateral to the CV.

- Origin Point of the Spleen
- Intersection Point of the Liver

- Intersection Point of the Yin Linking Vessel

This point is comparable to SP-12. The main difference is that it lies closer to the femoral nerve. This point can also be used as a neurological shutdown point.

Activation angle: 90°

SP-14: *Ujie* (Abdomen's Knot)

Located 3 cun above SP-13, 1.5 cun below SP-15, on the lateral side of the rectus abdominis, 4 cun lateral to the CV.

This point can shock the system and produce knock out. In order to do this, though, you will have to overcome the external oblique muscle which protects the point.

Activation angle: 90°

SP-15: *Aheng* (Big Horizontal)

4 cun lateral to the center of the umbilicus, on the mamillary line, lateral to the rectus abdominis, in the external and internal oblique and the transverse abdominis muscles.

- Origin Point of the Spleen

- Intersection Point of the Yin Linking Vessel

Although this point strike will cause things like diarrhea instantly and great nausea, it is too well protected by the external oblique muscles which, in this area can be built up to great proportions.

Activation angle: 90°

SP-16: *Uai* (Abdomen's Sorrow)

3 cun above SP-15, 4 cun lateral to the CV.

This point is located near the diaphragm.

- Origin Point of the Spleen

- Intersection Point of the Yin Linking Vessel

A powerful strike may be fatal due to suffocation. At the very least it may knock the breath from the opponent.

Activation angle: 90°

SP-17: *Hidou* (Food's Cavity)

6 cun lateral to the CV, or 2 cun lateral to the mammillary line, in the 5th intercostal space.

Localized pain may persist for several hours after striking. A hard strike may cause cardiac arrest. In order to accomplish this, the arm must be elevated to allow for the penetration of the strike.

Activation angle: 45°

SP-18: *Ianxi* (Heaven's Stream)

2 cun lateral to the nipple or 6 cun lateral to the CV, in the 4th intercostal space.

A strike may cause shock rising upward to the head and will drain the energy. A more powerful strike may also effect cardiac arrest. Even light finger pressure will cause great localized pain.

Activation angle: 45°

SP-19: *Iongxiang* (Chest Home)

1 rib above SP-18, in the 3rd intercostal space, 6 cun lateral to the CV.

This point can affect the opposite leg, realizing a cross-body motor reflex to occur.

Great nerve damage can be realized to the shoulder area.

Activation angle: 45°

SP-20: *Hourong* (Encircling Glory)

1 rib above SP-19, directly below LU-1, in the 2nd intercostal space, 6 cun lateral to the CV.

This point may also affect the way the opposite leg functions in a diminished fashion.

It can cause localized damage to tendons in the shoulder when struck.

This point is often employed with LV-14 with lethal results. Such a combination may cause respiratory and cardiac result to ensue.

Activation angle: 45°

SP-21: *Abao* (Big Wrapping)

On the mid-axillary line, 6 cun below the axilla, midway between the axilla and the free end of the 11th rib, in the 7th intercostal space.

- Frees the channels, Quickens the Connecting Vessels
- Exit Point

This point can wreck havoc on the energetic system of the body. A hard strike can even cause coma.

Liver damage can result from powerful strikes. Due to its connection with LU-1, it can also damage the lungs. The lungs may collapse and cause suffocation.

Due to its location over the ribs, the ribs can be broken if the strike is made perpendicular to the body.

If this point is used in conjunction with ST-9. knockout may occur and the spleen can be damaged.

Activation angle: 45°

Chapter 10

The Stomach Meridian

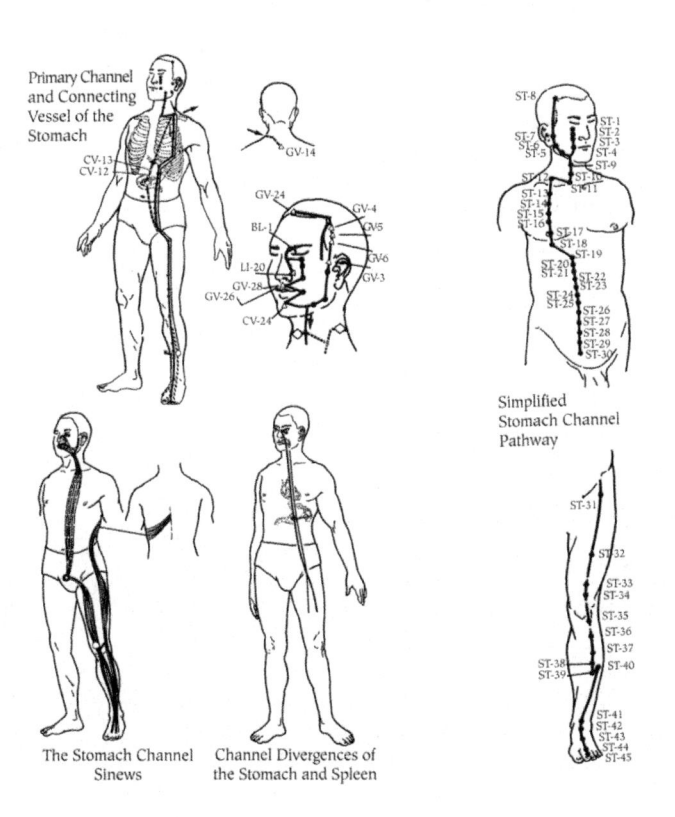

Stomach Meridian Overview	
Element	Earth
This element creates	Metal
This element attacks	Water
Polarity	Yang / Bowel
Coupled Meridian	Spleen
Connecting Points	ST-40 & SP-3
Active Time	7:00 to 9:00 pm
Entry Point	ST-1
Exit Point	ST-42
Sedation Point	ST-45
Tonification Point	ST-41
Alarm Point	CV-12
Associated Point	BL-21
Source Point	ST-42
Horary Point	ST-36
Metal / Well Point	ST-45
Water / Spring Point	ST-44
Wood / Stream Point	ST-43
Fire / River Point	ST-41
Earth / Sea Point	ST-36
Meridian Connections	GV-24
	GV-14
	CV-12
	CV-13
	ST-30

GENERAL/ELEMENTAL QUALITIES:

The functions of the Stomach fu are to control the 'rotting and ripening' of food, to control descending and to act as the first stage in the digestion of fluids. Disharmony of the Stomach therefore manifests as disorders of appetite and digestion, distention and pain in the epigastrium due to failure of the Stomach qi to descend, or belching, nausea or vomiting due to rebellious ascent of Stomach qi. In the Chinese tradition the 'sage faces South', and thus the light and warmth of the sun fall on the front of the body. The yangming channels on the anterior of the limbs receives the full intensity of the sun, as does the abdominal and chest portion of the foot yangming Stomach channel, the only yang channel to run along the anterior of the body. For this reason, yangming or 'yang brightness' is considered to be particularly full of yang qi. Points of the Stomach channel, therefore, are among the most important points to clear excess of yang in the form of febrile heat, or heat which rises to disturb the Heart and spirit. As yang ming descends so does shao yin ascend.

GREATER VESSEL: The Stomach channel starts from the lateral side of ala nasi at LI-20. It ascends along the nose and meets the Bladder channel at

Jingming BL-1 where it proceeds to ST-1 and descends and deviates medially to meet with both GV-28 and GV-26, circles around the lips and meets the Conception vessel at CV-24 in the mentolabial groove of the chin, runs laterally across the cheeks to ST-5 and ST-6 at the angle of the mandible, then enters the upper gums. It passes upward to ST-8 via GB-3, 4, 5, 6 and continues with a branch to GV-24. At ST-5 it descends down the neck to ST-12 (a branch also goes back to GV-14 and from there descends along the GV) along the anterior aspect of the thorax in the mammary line 4 cun from midline. In abdomen it continues down 2 cun from midline and down anterior aspect of leg to the lateral aspect of the middle toe. A brancy involving the Pylorus descends to connect with the main channel at ST-30.

TENDINO MUSCULAR MERIDIAN: ST-45 to SI-18

DIVERGENT CHANNEL (DISTINCT MERIDIAN): ST-30, LV-12 to ST-1

LONGITUDINAL LUO CHANNEL: ST-37

TRANSVERSE LUO CHANNEL: ST-37 to LV-3

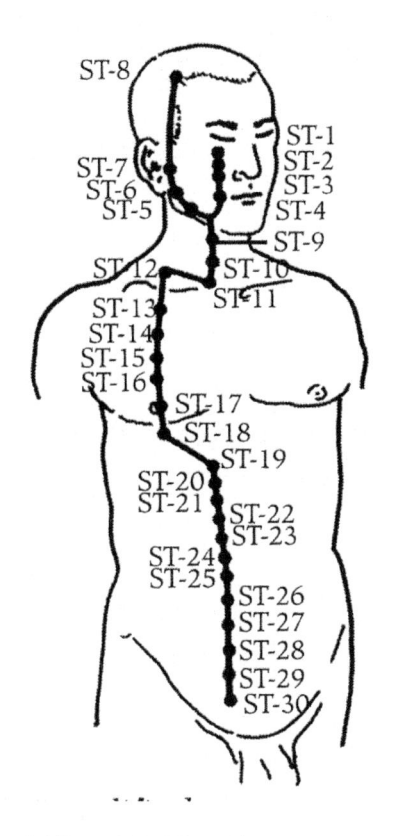

ST-1: *Chengqi* (Contain Tears)

Between the eyeball and the midpoint of the infraorbital ridge. The point is above the inferior border of the orbit, in the orbicularis oculi muscle, and in its deep position, within the orbit are the rectus inferior bulbi and the obliques Inferior bulbi muscles.

- Origin Point of the Stomach
- Intersection Point of the Yang Motility Vessel
- Entry Point

This point is extremely sensitive and is vulnerable to even a light power strike, even causing nausea. This point may also drain energy from the upper body.

Medium power strikes often cause knock out. Harder strikes may prove fatal.

This point is associated with LI-20 and will drain Yang Qi from the body.

The liver may also be affected.

Activation angle: 90°

ST-2: *Sibai* (Four Whites)

Approximately 1 cun directly below ST 1. In the Infraorbital foramen between the orbicularis oculi and quadratus labii superior muscles.

This point has been known to damage the nervous system and will drain energy resulting in knock out. The energy will drain downwards out of the legs.

Activation angle: 90°

ST-3: *Juliao* (Great Seam)

Located directly below ST-2, at the level of the lower border of the ala nasi, on the lateral side of the nasolabial groove.

- Origin Point of the Stomach
- Intersection Point of the Large Intestine
- Intersection Point of the Yang Motility Vessel

A strike can disrupt the brain and can cause disorientation and nausea.

Activation angle: 45°

ST-4: *Dicang* (Earth Granary)

Lateral to the corner of the mouth, directly below ST-3, in the orbicularis oris muscle and in its deep position. In the buccinator muscle.

- Origin Point of the Stomach

- Intersection Point of the Large Intestine

- Intersection Point of the Yang Motility Vessel

- Frees the channels

- Quickens the Connecting Vessels

Hard strikes may result in knock out. Medium power strikes may shock the entire system.

Activation angle: 15°

ST-5: *Dayying* (Big Welcome, or Big Meeting)

Anterior to the angle of the mandible, on the anterior border of the masseter muscle, in the groove like depression appearing when the cheek is bulged 0.5 cun anterior to ST-6.

A strike to the jaw here will disrupt the brain and can cause dizziness and confusion. Strikes here are able to send a lot of Yang Qi into the brain.

A medium power strike may result in knock out while a more powerful strike can break the jaw.

This point is also associated with ST-9 by way of ST-1 and ST-8. Its correlation with ST-9 will cause knock out via the carotid sinus stopping the blood pressure. Moreover, there are vagus nerve endings that enter the base of the stomach.

Activation angle: 45°

ST-6: *Jiache* (Jaw Vehicle)

One finger breadth anterior and superior to the lower angle of the mandible where the masseter attaches at the prominence of the muscle when the teeth are clenched.

- Frees the channels
- Quickens the Connecting Vessels

This point will often result in an easy knock out. This point is a neurological shutdown point which can affect the brain patterns.

Hard strikes here may cause concussion, nausea, and amnesia.

Activation angle: 15°

ST-7: *Xiaguan* (Lower Hinge)

In the depression at the lower border of the zygomatic arch, anterior to the condyloid process of the mandible, located with the mouth closed.

Below this point is the parotid gland and the origin of the masseter muscle.

- Intersection Point of the Gall Bladder
- Origin Point of the Stomach
- Drains Fire

This point is known to drain energy. Accurate strikes may induce knock out. The drainage will drain energy down the body and out of the legs.

Activation angle: 90°

ST-8: *Touwei* (Head Support) (Head Safeguard)

Located 0.5 cun within the anterior hairline at the corner of the forehead. 4.5cun lateral to the GV. The point is found in the galea aponeurotica on the superior margin of the temporalis muscle.

- Intersection Point of the Gall Bladder
- Origin Point of the Stomach
- Intersection Point of the Yang Linking Vessel

This point may cause concussion with more nausea than any of the other head strikes. Great localized pain may be experienced with drainage of energy, followed by knock out. Death may occur when this strike is hard enough.

Activation angle: 15°

ST-9: *Renying* (Man's Welcome)

Level with the t1p of the Adam's apple, just on the course of the common carotid artery, on the anterior, border of the sternocleidomastoideus muscle In the platysma muscle. 1.5cun lateral to the laryngeal prominence at the meeting of the anterior margin of sternocieldomastoid and the thyroid cartilage.

- Intersection Point of the Gall Bladder
- Origin Point of the Stomach
- Four Seas Point: Sea of Qi
- Window of the Sky Point
- Associated with an Extraordinary Vessel of the Yin Motility Vessel
- One of 36 Vital Points Listed in the Bubishi

This point lies along the vagus sinus, artery and nerve. It can cause anything from extreme pain to death. It will easily affect a knock out.

The carotid sinus is known to be baroreceptor. It detects changes in blood pressure. When a change is detected, a signal is sent via the vagus nerve to the vasomotor center (Located in the medulla oblongata. It regulates blood pressure via the autonomic nervous system.) in the brain. As a result, vasodilation (a widening of a blood vessel) results and the heart rate occurs, causing the blood pressure to lower. This phenomenon is known as carotid sinus reflex.

Activation angle: 90°

ST-10: *Shuitu* (Water Prominence)

At the anterior border of the sternocleidomastoideus, midway between ST-9 and ST-11.

This point is comparable in danger to ST-9 and may even be more dangerous. A strike may cause Yang Qi to rush into the head causing knock out.

This point is often employed in conjunction with PC-6.

Activation angle: 90°

ST-11: *Qishe* (Qi's Residence)

At the superior border of the sternal extremity of the clavicle, between the sternal head and the clavicular head of the sternocleidomastoideus muscle, directly below ST-9.

This point could be considered a sort of "switch" for the heart. If the heart is active, it may cause cardiac arrest. If the heart has already stopped, this point may restart the heart. I have personally experienced this phenomena in my school when Grandmaster Rick Moneymaker was able to restart the heart of a student's father when he went into cardiac arrest moments before. His heart was instantly restarted from thumb pressure into the point.

This point is often coupled with strikes to ST-15 and ST-16.

Activation angle: 90°

ST-12: *Quepen* (Empty Basin)

In the midpoint of the supraclavicular fossa, 4 cun lateral to the CV or in the depression at the middle of the superior border of the clavicle and directly above the nipple.

- Lowers the blood pressure

- Associated with an Extraordinary Vessel of the Yin Motility vessel

- One of 36 Vital Points Listed in the Bubishi

Striking this point robs the opponent of the will to fight. A medium power strike is capable of breaking the clavicle.

This point is known to affect the communication between the upper and lower halves of the body.

Due to its connection with GV-14, the meeting place of Yang, this point may drain energy from the whole body.

It is often coupled with ST-11 to effect massive drainage of energy.

Activation angle: 90°

ST-13: *Qihu* (Qi's Household)

At the middle of the inferior border of the clavicle, on the mamillary line (4 cun lateral to the CV MO).

Whereas ST 12 drains qi, ST 13 adds Yang qi to the head causing loss of balance to the falling down point. With most of the ST points, it will also cause great nausea. This is one of those points where the qi is said to enter the meridian, so a strike here also unbalances the yin and yang energy in the whole body.

Activation angle: 90°

ST-14: *Kufang* (Storehouse)

In the first intercostal space, on the mamillary line, 4 cun lateral to CV-20.

Striking this point hard often leads to nausea.

Activation angle: 45°

ST-15: *Wuyi* (Room screen)

In the 2nd intercostal space, on the mamillary line, 4 cun lateral to CV-19.

This point can stop the heart if struck hard enough or in combination with ST-16.

Activation angle: 45°

ST-16: *Yingghuan* (Breast's Window)

In the 3rd intercostal space, on the mamillary line, 4cun lateral to CV-18.

Comparable to ST-15.

Activation angle: 45°

ST-17: *Ruzhong* (Middle of Breast)

In the middle of the nipple In the 4th intercostal space.

Medium power strikes have the capacity of being lethal here. The point requires extreme accuracy to have that affect though. This point will drain energy and may result in a loss of memory. More powerful strikes are said to lead to mental illness.

Activation angle: 45°

ST-18: *Rugen* (Breast Root)

In the 5th intercostal space, directly below the nipple.

This point requires a powerful strike to show any result. You will often see LV-14 used in conjunction with a strike here, resulting in greater energy drainage.

Activation angle: 45°

ST-19: *Burong* (Uncontainable)

6 cun above the umbilicus, 2cun lateral to CV-14.

Similar in effect to CV-17, this point attacks the seat of power of the body. It can injure the diaphragm. More powerful strikes can cause death from suffocation.

Activation angle: 45°

ST-20: *Chengman* (Support Fullness)

5 cun above the umbilicus, 2 cun lateral to CV-13 and 1 cun below ST-19.

Comparable to ST-19.

Activation angle: 90°

ST-21: *Liangmen* (Door of the Beam)

4 cun above the umbilicus, 2 cun lateral to the CV-12.

This point is a little more difficult to get to due to being covered by the abdominal muscles. A hard strike will penetrate through the muscle and activate the point though.

A lot of localized pain may be experienced. Energy often drains and causes stomach and spleen problems. Affects the Yang Qi.

Activation angle: 90°

ST-22: *Guanmen* (Gate)

3 cun above the umbilicus, 2 cun lateral to CV-11.

This point may disrupt the communication between the upper and lower halves of the body, the heaven and the earth. It is known to drain the lower body primarily.

Activation angle: 90°

ST-23: *Taiyi* (Great Yi)

2 cun above the umbilicus, 2 cun lateral to CV-10.

Comparable to ST-22. In addition, it may cause bladder problems and may cause urination when struck using an accurate strike.

Activation angle: 90°

ST-24: *Huaroumen* (Door of Slippery Flesh)

Located 1 cun above the umbilicus, 2 cun lateral to CV-9.

This point is difficult to get to due to being protected by the abdominal muscles. It can affect the large intestine and colon. A hard strike is said to cause immediate defecation.

Activation angle: 90°

ST-25: *Tianshu* (Heaven's Axis)

2 cun lateral to the center of the umbilicus. Located directly above the colon.

- Alarm Point of the Large Intestine
- Regulates the Spleen and Stomach

This is the alarm point of the large intestine. There is little physical protection at this point from the abdominal muscles.

Struck hard, knock out may result. Also, gastrointestinal problems may result along with emotional problems due to its effect on the balance between the Shen and the Gall Bladder and Triple Burner.

Activation angle: 90°

ST-26: *Wailing* (Outer Tomb)

1 cun below the umbilicus, 2 cun lateral to CV-7.

Comparable to ST-25 in result. It is located directly above the colon, the same as ST-25.

Hard strikes may result in knock out.

Activation angle: 90°

ST-27: *Daju* (The Great or, Big Huge)

2 cun below the umbilicus, 2 cun lateral to CV-5.

This is a Shokanten point of Yang Ming and as such the strike will disrupt the communication between the Shen (Spirit) and Large Intestine and Stomach.

Emotional problems may be immediately experienced

Localized pain and energy loss are the normal reaction to a strike. Harder strikes may result in knock out.

Activation angle: 90°

ST-28: *Shuidao* (Water Way)

3 cun below the umbilicus, 2 cun lateral to GV-4. In the rectus abdominis muscle and its sheath.

This is a dangerous point. It may immediately cause knock out through the action on the Large Intestine affecting the lower heater which will expand outwards to the rest of the lower abdomen. This point can shock the whole lower heater, causing damage to the elimination system.

Activation angle: 90°

ST-29: *Guilai* (Return)

4 cun below the umbilicus. 2 cun lateral to CV-3. In the lateral margin of the rectus abdominis muscle, the internal oblique muscle and the aponeurosis of the transverse abdomens muscle.

It is located near CV-3 which is the meeting point of the three yin meridians of the region. It can stagnate energy.

The point may cause knock out. A harder strike may be lethal.

Activation angle: 90°

ST-30: *Qichong* (Pouring QI)

5 cun below the umbilicus, 2 cun lateral to CV-2, superior to the inguinal groove, on the medial side of the femoral artery. In the aponeurosis of the external and internal oblique muscles, and the lower region of the transverse abdominis muscle.

- Origin Point of the Stomach
- Four Seas Point: Upper Sea of Water and Grain

This is the Sea of Nourishment Point along with ST 36. It is also a point of the Penetrating Vessel. It circulates Source Qi to the stomach.

A strike may lower the body's immunity. The flow of energy is also hindered.

A medium power strike may result in knock out, while a harder blow may be fatal.

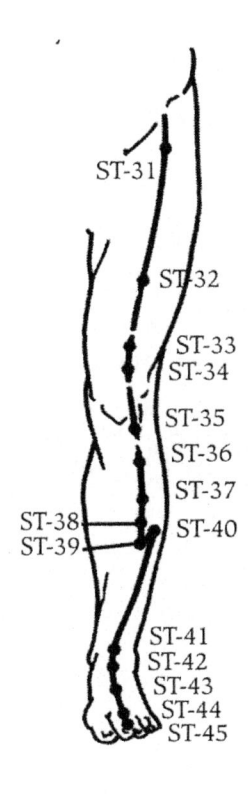

Activation angle: 45°

ST-31: *Biguan* (Hip Hinge or Thigh Gate)

Directly below the anterior superior iliac spine, in the depression on the lateral side of the sartorius muscle when the thigh is flexed, level with the perineum. Inferior and medial to the great trochanter of the femur, between the sartorius and the tensor fascia lata muscles.

This point is known to drain the energy of the legs.

Activation angle: 90°

ST-32: *Futu* (Hidden Rabbit)

6 cun above the laterosuperior border of the patella, on the line connecting the anterior superior iliac spine and the lateral border of the patella. At the lateral, anterior aspect of the femur, in the middle of the belly of the rectus femoris muscle.

This point may paralyze the legs temporarily like ST-31 does. A hard strike may result in knock out due to the simulated effects of shock that occur from striking this point.

Activation angle: 90°

ST-33: *Yinshi* (Yin's Market)

3 cun above the laterosuperior border of the patella, on the line connecting the anterior superior iliac spine and the lateral border of the patella.

This point causes localized pain. It can send energy to the head leading to confusion and even knock out to occur if struck hard enough.

Activation angle: 90°

ST-34: *Liangqiu* (Ridge Mould OR Beam Mound)

2 cun above the laterosuperior border of the patella, between the rectus femoris and the vastus lateralis muscles of the thigh.

- Regulates the Spleen and Stomach
- Cleft-xi Point

This is a xi-cleft point which stores Zhen Qi. When struck, it disrupts qi and blood.

Localized pain results with a loss of leg strength.

Activation angle: 15°

ST-35: *Dubi* (Calf Nose) or *Xiyan* (Eyes of Knee)

When The knee is flexed, the point is in the depression below the patella and lateral to the patella tendon.

This point may severely drain energy in the Kidney resulting in extreme fatigue.

Activation angle: 15°

ST-36: *Zusanli* (Three Measures of the Leg)

3 cun below ST-35, one finger breadth from the anterior crest of the tibia. Between the tibialis anterior and the tendon of the extensor digitorum longus pedis.

- Lower Uniting-He Point of the Stomach
- Earth Point
- Uniting-He Point
- Frees the channels
- Quickens the Connecting Vessels
- Regulates the Spleen and Stomach
- Rectifies Qi

- Lowers the blood pressure
- Command Point of the abdomen
- Horary Point
- Four Seas Point: Lower Sea of Water and Grain

This point is an earth and he point and sea of nourishment point along with ST-30.

A strike may cause overall system weakness and can damage the spleen.

Activation angle: 90°

ST-37: *Shangjuxu* (Upper Void)

Located on the lower leg 3 cun below ST-36, in the tibialis anterior muscle.

- Lower Uniting-He Point of the Large Intestine
- Uniting-He Point of the Large Intestine
- Regulates the Spleen and Stomach
- Four Seas Point: Sea of Blood

This point can damage the function of the colon causing defecation immediately if struck hard enough.

It may also fill the legs with too much energy causing an imbalance in the whole system and can affect the Wei Qi, or protecting energy, weakening the immune system.

Activation angle: 90°

ST-38: *Tiakou* (Line's Opening)

8 cun below ST-35, 2 cun below ST-37, midway between ST-35 and ST-41.

- Frees the channels
- Quickens the Connecting Vessels

This point can affect the shoulders. It can drain the arms of energy.

Activation angle: 90°

ST-39: *Xiajuxu* (Lower Void)

9 cun below ST-35, 3 cun below ST-37, one finger breadth out from the anterior crest of the tibia.

- Lower Uniting-He Point of the Small Intestine
- Uniting-He Point of the Small Intestine
- Four Seas Point: Sea of Blood

This point affects the Small Intestine and may cause paralysis of the legs when struck hard. In addition it may injure the Wei qi and cause problems with the immune system.

Localized pain is experienced when struck.

Activation angle: 90°

ST-40: *Fenglong* (Abundance and Prosperity)

Located 8 cun superior and anterior to the external malleolus, about 1 finger breadth posterior or lateral to ST-8, between the lateral side of the extensor digitorum longus pedis and the peroneus brevis muscles.

- Connecting-luo Point of the Spleen
- Regulates the Spleen and Stomach
- Rectifies Qi
- Lowers the blood pressure

This point has an affect upon the Spleen. It may imbalance the Stomach and Spleen and weaken the body.

Activation angle: 90°

ST-41: *Jiexi* (Release Stream)

At the junction of the dorsum of the foot and the leg, between the tendons of the extensor digitorum longus and hallucis longus, approximately at the level of the tip of the external malleolus.

- Fire Point
- River-jing Point
- Regulates the Spleen and Stomach
- Tonification Point

This is a fire and jing point and will affect the stomach causing nausea. It may drain energy from the lower body causing the legs to become weak.

Activation angle: 15°

ST-42: *Chongyang* (Pouring Yang)

Distal to ST-41, at the highest point of the dorsum of the foot, in the depression between the 2nd and 3rd metatarsal bones and the cuneiform bone.

- Source Point
- Exit Point

The strike may cause nerve damage. This is a source point and may cause significant energy loss and localized pain.

Activation angle: 15°

ST-43: *Xiangru* (Sinking Valley)

In the depression distal to the junction of the 2nd and 3rd metatarsal bones, directly above the lateral side of the 2nd toe.

- Wood Point
- Stream-shu Point
- Destructive Point

This is a wood and shu point. This point disrupts the free flow of energy when struck and drains it.

Activation angle: 15°

ST-44: *Netting* (Inner Court)

Proximal to the web margin between the 2nd and 3rd toes, in the depression distal and lateral to the 2nd metatarsodigital joint.

- Spring-ying Point
- Water Point
- Frees the channels, Quickens the Connecting Vessels
- Regulates the Spleen and Stomach

Striking this point may cause localized pain and disrupt the energy enough to cause knock out if struck hard enough.

Activation angle: 15°

ST-45: *Lidui* (Strict Exchange)

On the lateral side of the 2nd toe, about 0.1 cun posterior to the corner of the nail.

- Well-jing Point
- Metal Point

- Sedation Point

This is a metal and cheng point. It affects the muscles and tendons.

When attacked, confusion may result. In some cases, even nose bleed has been experienced.

Activation angle: 15°

Chapter 11
The Kidney Meridian

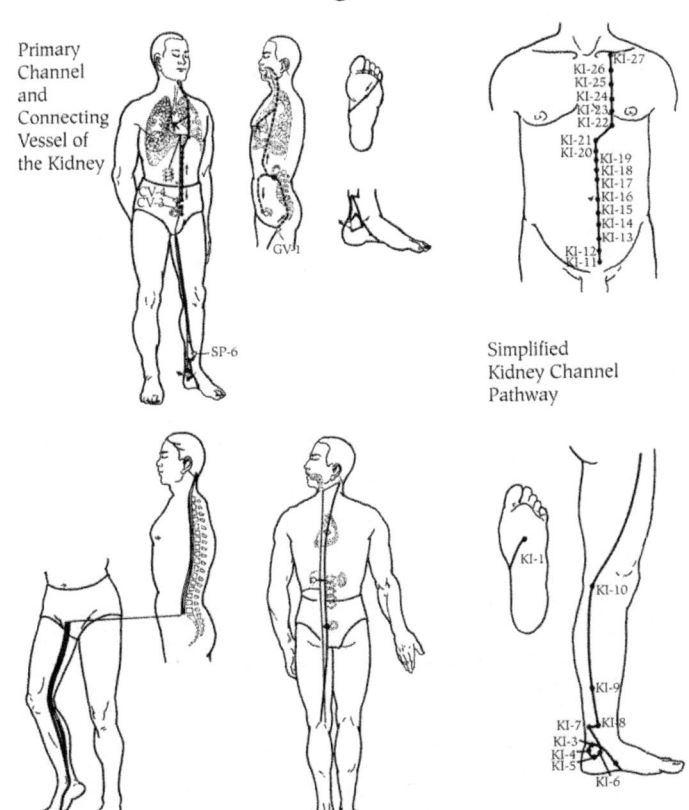

Primary Channel and Connecting Vessel of the Kidney

Simplified Kidney Channel Pathway

The Kidney Channel Sinews

Channel Divergences of the Kidney and Bladder

Kidney Meridian Overview	
Element	Water
This element creates	Wood
This element attacks	Fire
Polarity	Yin / Organ
Coupled Meridian	Bladder
Connecting Points	KI-4 & BL-64
Active Time	5:00 to 7:00 pm
Entry Point	KI-1
Exit Point	KI-22
Sedation Point	KI-1
Tonification Point	KI-7
Alarm Point	GB-25
Associated Point	BL-23
Source Point	KI-3
Horary Point	KI-10
Wood / Well Point	KI-1
Fire / Spring Point	KI-2
Earth / Stream Point	KI-3
Metal / River Point	KI-7
Water / Sea Point	KI-10
Meridian Connections	CV-3, 4, 7, 17 GV-1 KI-9 (Yin linking) KI-3

The Kidneys have five principal functions:
- storing essence and dominating reproduction, growth and development.
- producing marrow, filling up the brain, dominating bones and assisting in the production of blood.
- dominating Water.
- controlling the reception of qi.
- opening into the ears and dominating the two lower yin (the anus and urethra).

GREATER VESSEL: Begins beneath the little toe and crosses the sole of the foot to Yongquan KI-1, it ascends along the medial aspect of the leg following the points of the Meridian. It connects with SP-6, and from KI-10 follows the postero-medial aspect of the thigh to the tip of the coccyx where it intersects with GV-l. From there it ascends through the spine, enters the zang Kidney and connects with the fu Bladder, from whence it follow up the anterior aspect of abdomen and chest to just below the clavicle at KI-27.

One branch emerges from the Kidney, ascends through the Liver and diaphragm, enters the Lung and ascends along the throat to terminate at the root of the tongue, while another branch separates in the Lung, joins with the Heart and disperses in the chest to link with the Pericardium Meridian at CV-17.

TENDINO MUSCULAR MERIDIAN: Follows the KI meridian but involves genitals and sends a branch vetebrae which acends to the occipital bone emerging at SI-18.

DIVERGENT CHANNEL (DISTINCT MERIDIAN): KI-10, BL-40 to BL-10 passing through the rectum, uterus, prostate, kidney, bladder up to the nape of the neck passing via the root of the toungue.

LONGITUDINAL LUO CHANNEL: From KI-4 sends feeders out to the heel and goes up BL meridian of leg to connect with KI meridian of abdomen, connects with the pericardium organ and then sends branches back to the lumbar vertebrae.

TRANSVERSE LUO CHANNEL: KI-4 to BL-64

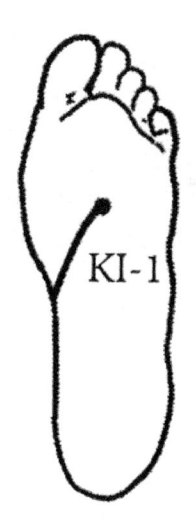

KI-1: *Yongquan* (Gushing Spring)

In the depression appearing on the sole of the foot when the foot is in plantar flexion, approximately at the junction of the anterior and middle third when the sole is divided into thirds from the base of the 2nd toe to the heel. The point is between the 2nd and 3rd metatarsal bones in the aponeurosis of the sole; medial to the point are the tendons of the flexor digitorum pedis, longus and brevis, and the 2nd lubricalis pedis muscle. In its deep position it lies in the interossei plantares muscle.

- Well-jing Point
- Wood Point
- Lowers the blood pressure

- Entry Point

- Sedation Point

This point stores energy and can be used in an emergency to release the energy stored there.

It is often employed in Martial Arts stances to stimulate the energetic system, especially the Cat Stance or Crane Stance.

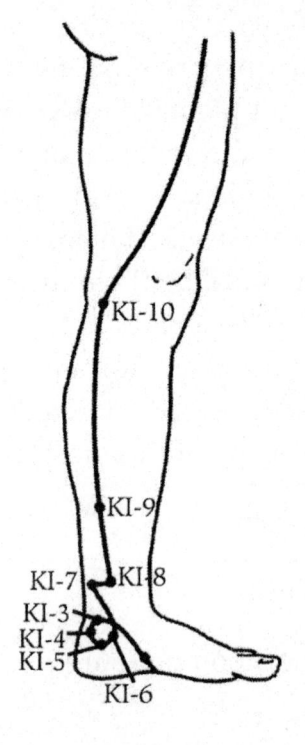

Activation angle: 90°

KI-2: *Rangu* (Burning Valley)

Anterior and inferior to the medial malleolus, in the depression on the lower border of the tuberosity of the navicular bone, anterior and inferior to joint of the navicular, in the abductor halluces muscle.

- Spring-ying Point
- Fire Point
- Downbears Fire
- Sedation Point

This is a fire and spring or stream point. All spring points can do great damage to the body.

Localized pain is common from a strike. The bowels may also be affected in an adverse way, making the stool loose.

This is the Fire point on a Water meridian and as such, may imbalance the Yin and Yang greatly within the energetic system. Especially the Kidney Yang may be weakened and lead to a weakening of the entire body.

Activation angle: 90°

KI-3: *Taixi* (Great Creek / Bigger Stream)

In the depression between the medial malleolus and the tendo calcaneus, level with the tip of the medial malleolus.

- Source Point
- Stream-shu Point
- Earth Point
- Lowers the blood pressure

This is a very painful point. It can drain energy and cause knock out. It is often coupled with KI-10.

This point weakens Kidney Jing and can inhibit the Kidney's action of storing energy.

Activation angle: 45°

KI-4: *Dazhong* (Big Goblet)

Posterior and inferior to the medial malleolus. In the depression medial to the attachment of the tendo-calcaneus.

- Connecting-luo Point of the Bladder
- Rectifies the Spleen

When struck, this point may obstruct and hinder the energy's flow throughout the body, and the Yang organs in particular.

Activation angle: 45°

KI-5: *Shuiquan* (Spring)

1 cun directly below KI-3, in the depression anterior and superior to the medial side of the tuberosity of the calcaneum.

- Cleft-xi Point
- Destructive Point

This is a Xie cleft point and as such in the healing area will clear blockages by inserting a great amount of qi into the system. However, when struck using adverse qi, this point will cause instant qi drainage, thus causing the recipient to fall down. Local pain is great with this strike.

Activation angle: 15°

KI-6: *Zhaohai* (Shining Sea)

1 cun below the medial malleolus of the ankle, at the insertion of the abductor hallucis muscle.

- Origin Point of the Kidney
- Intersection Point of the Yin Motility vessel
- Confluence Point of Yin Motility Vessel
- Master Point of the Yin Motility vessel
- Coupled Point with Extraordinary Meridian of the Conception Vessel
- Associated with an Extraordinary Vessel of the Yin Motility vessel
- One of 36 Vital Points Listed in the Bubishi

A painful point to strike with lots of localized pain.

It is the Master Point for the Yin Heel Vessel, which is coupled with the Conception Vessel. When struck, it causes massive energy drainage to occur.

Activation angle: 90°

KI-7: *Fuliu* (Returning Column / Current)

2 cun directly above KI-3, on the anterior border of the tendo calcaneus, posterior to the tibia. at the inferior part of the soleus muscle and in the medial part of the calcaneous.

- River-jing Point

- Metal Point
- Downbears Fire
- Absorb Qi
- Tonification Point

This is a metal and jing point. When struck it often damages the Kidneys, especially it's Jing.

Rising Heat to the head which occurs as a result of a strike often causes knock out and extreme nausea.

The point also affects the Lungs and drains energy from the body.

Activation angle: 90°

KI-8: *Jiaoxin* (Crossing Letters)

2 cun above KI-3. 0.5 cun anterior to KI-7, posterior to the medial border of the tibia.

- Origin Point of the Kidney
- Intersection Point of the Yin Motility vessel
- Cleft-xi Point

This point is often struck simultaneously with KI-7 and can lead to confusion and insomnia.

Activation angle: 90°

KI-9: *Zhubin* (House Guest)

On a line drawn between KI-3 and KI-10, this point is located about 5 cun above KI-3, at the lower end of the belly of the gastrocnemius around 2 cun posterior to the medial margin of the tibia. Where the gastrocnemius forms the calcaneus tendon, under the soleus muscle.

- Origin Point of the Kidney
- Intersection Point of the Yin Linking Vessel
- Cleft-xi Point

This is a Xie-cleft point, or accumulation point. Because of this, energy damage is often great.

It can cause intense localized pain when struck. Strikes often injure the kidneys. Harder strikes may cause knock out, especially when used in combinations.

Activation angle: 90°

KI-10: *Yingu* (Yin's Valley)

On the medial side of the popliteal fossa, level with BL-40, between the tendons of semitendinosus and semimembranosus when the knee is flexed.

- Uniting-He Point
- Water Point
- Horary Point

Water and he point. It is a very dangerous point.

Striking this point may cause the kidneys to fail. It attacks the "seat of power" of the body via its connection with the Conception Vessel through CV-17.

Knockout is likely from powerful strikes.

The heart is often affected by strikes as well. In addition, the Girdle Vessel is highly affected by strikes to this point, which can cause an imbalance between heaven and earth, or the upper and lower halves of the body.

Activation angle: 90°

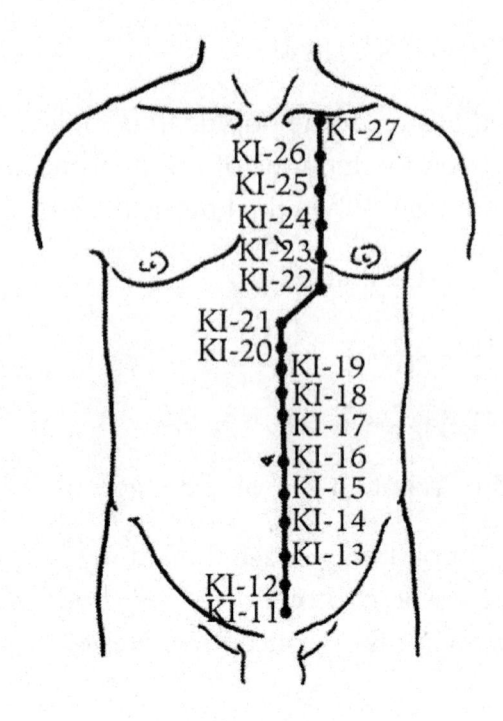

KI-11: *Henggu* (Horizontal Bone)

5 cun below the umbilicus, on the superior border of the symphysis pubis, 0.5 cun lateral to CV-2.

- Origin Point of the Kidney
- Intersection Point of the Penetrating Vessel

This is the first of the Kidney points which connects to the Penetrating Vessel, which also known as the life force meridian.

In addition, this point connects with the Conception Vessel and affects the lower heater.

The kidneys are directly affected from strikes and can cause localized pain and even knock out.

Activation angle: 90°

KI-12: *Dahe* (Great Clarity)

4 cun below the umbilicus, 0.5 cun lateral to CV-3.
Innervation: The branches of the subcostal nerve and the iliohypogastric nerve.

- Origin Point of the Kidney
- Intersection Point of the Penetrating Vessel

This point can affect the emotions and mental soundness, causing confusion.

It can also cause massive energy drainage from the body. Less powerful strikes cause localized pain. Harder strikes may lead to knock out.

Activation angle: 90°

KI-13: *Qixue* (Qi's Orifice)

3 cun below the umbilicus, 0.5 cun lateral to CV-4. Innervation: The subcostal nerve.

- Origin Point of the Kidney
- Intersection Point of the Penetrating Vessel

This point has little physical protection from strikes, making it extremely vulnerable to attack.

It can affect the Penetrating Vessel and affect the entire energetic system of the body.

Knock out is very common from strikes. More powerful strikes may be fatal.

Activation angle: 90°

KI-14: *Siman* (Four Full)

2 cun below the umbilicus, 0.5 cun lateral to CV-5. Innervation: The 11th intercostal nerve.

- Origin Point of the Kidney
- Intersection Point of the Penetrating Vessel

This point can attack the *tantien* via the Girdle Vessel. Hard strikes often cause knock out and even death within minutes after the knock out.

Activation angle: 90°

KI-15: *Zhongzhu* (Middle Flow)

1 cun below the umbilicus, 0.5 cun lateral to CV-7. Innervation: the 10 intercostal nerves. Irrigation is the same as for KI-12.

- Origin Point of the Kidney
- Intersection Point of the Penetrating Vessel

This point also affects the Penetrating Vessel. The effect on the *tantien* is less than the previous point however.

There is more protection at this point due to muscle covering the point.

Hard strikes may lead to an experience of suffocation from the energy that is made to rise to the neck area.

Activation angle: 90°

KI-16: *Huangshu* (Vital's Hollow)

0.5 cun lateral to the center of the umbilicus. Innervation: The 10th intercostal nerve and irrigation is the same as for KI-12.

- Origin Point of the Kidney
- Intersection Point of the Penetrating Vessel

This point is a Shokanten point of Shao Yin. When this point is struck, it may damage the Penetrating Vessel, leading to extreme fatigue. It can also cause great imbalance between Fire and Water.

Activation angle: 90°

KI-17: *Shangqu* (Trade's Bend)

Located 2 cun above the umbilicus, 0.5cun lateral to CV-10. Innervation: The 9th intercostal nerve and irrigated by the branches of the superior and inferior epigastric arteries and veins.

- Origin Point of the Kidney
- Intersection Point of the Penetrating Vessel

This point rapidly drains the energy from the body leading to knock out.

It can also expel the air from the lungs. Moreover, it can impair the blood, and impede its flow to the brain, leading to knock out.

A hard strike can be fatal.

Activation angle: 90°

KI-18: *Shiguan* (Stone Hinge)

3 cun above the umbilicus, 0.5 cun lateral to GV-11.

- Origin Point of the Kidney
- Intersection Point of the Penetrating Vessel

This point is also connected to the Penetrating Vessel. It can drain energy from the body upsetting the "seat of power."

It can also increase the amount of Yang energy going to the head, also leading to knock out.

Activation angle: 90°

KI-19: *Yindu* (Yin's Metropolis)

4 cun above the umbilicus, 0.5 cun lateral to CV-12.

- Origin Point of the Kidney

- Intersection Point of the Penetrating Vessel

This is a moderately dangerous point to strike as it leads to massive energy drainage. A strike can affect the entire body's energetic system, causing knock out and a loss of breath. An attack can impair the diaphragm. Stronger attacks can be fatal.

Activation angle: 90°

KI-20: *Futonggu* (Connecting Valley on the Abdomen)

Located 5 cun above the umbilicus, 0.5cun lateral to CV-13.

- Origin Point of the Kidney
- Intersection Point of the Penetrating Vessel

Comparable to KI-19, but slightly more dangerous.

Activation angle: 90°

KI-21: *Youmen* (Secluded Door / Pylorus)

6 cun above the umbilicus, 0.5 cun lateral to CV-14.

- Origin Point of the Kidney

- Intersection Point of the Penetrating Vessel

This point is dangerous due to its location near the solar plexus and its connection with the Penetrating Vessel. It can cause cardiac arrest. It is very dangerous to strike during the time of the heart, or from 11:00 am to 1:00 pm. If struck at this time, the likelihood of death increases substantially.

Activation angle: 45°

KI-22: *Bulang* (Stepping Corridor)

In the 5th intercostal space, 2 cun lateral to the CV, approximately level to CV-16.

- Exit Point

Very comparable to KI-21, but slightly less dangerous.

Activation angle: 45°

KI-23: *Shenfeng* (Spirit's Seal)

In the 4th intercostal space, 2 cun lateral to CV-17.

This point affects the Shen, or spirit.

Strikes may cause cardiac arrest if struck hard enough.

Activation angle: 45°

KI-24: *Lingxu* (Spirit's Ruins)

In the 3rd intercostal space, 2 cun lateral to CV-18.

Comparable to KI-23.

Activation angle: 45°

KI-25: *Shencang* (Spirit's Storage)

In the 2nd intercostal space, 2 cun lateral to CV-19.

This point may affect the lungs and Shen, weakening the body. It scatters the energy when struck.

Activation angle: 45°

KI-26: *Yuzhong* (Amid Elegance)

In the first intercostal space, 2 cun lateral to CV-20.

Similar to KI-25 since it affects the energy of the lungs. It can cause a knock out even from pressure.

Activation angle: 45°

KI-27: *Shufu* (Hollow Residence)

In the depression at the lower border of the clavicle, 2 cun lateral to CV-21

This point drains energy from the body and can cause knock out if struck hard enough. Strikes may also impair communication between the two sides of the body, left and right.

Activation angle: 45°

Chapter 12

The Bladder Meridian

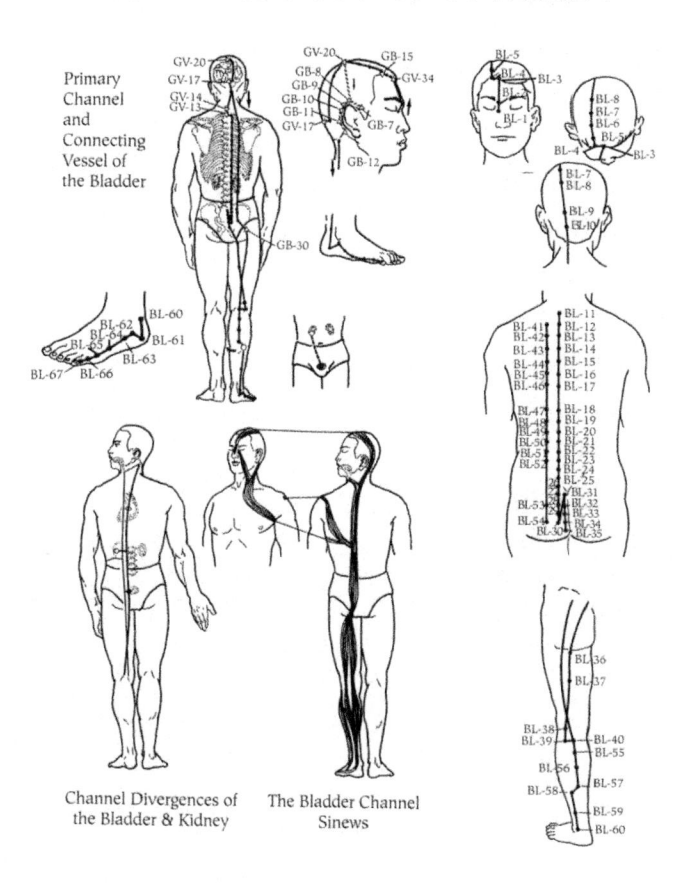

Primary Channel and Connecting Vessel of the Bladder

Channel Divergences of the Bladder & Kidney

The Bladder Channel Sinews

Bladder Meridian Overview	
Element	Water
This element creates	Wood
This element attacks	Fire
Polarity	Yang / Bowel
Coupled Meridian	Kidney
Connecting Points	BL-58 & KI-3
Active Time	3:00 to 5:00 pm
Entry Point	BL-1
Exit Point	BL-67
Sedation Point	BL-65
Tonification Point	BL-67
Alarm Point	CV-3
Associated Point	BL-28
Source Point	BL-64
Horary Point	BL-66
Metal / Well Point	BL-67
Water / Spring Point	BL-66
Wood / Stream Point	BL-65
Fire / River Point	BL-60
Earth / Sea Point	BL-40

GREATER VESSEL: The Bladder channel starts at the inner canthus of the eye. It ascends the forehead and joins the Governing Vessel at the point Baihui (DU 20). From here a branch goes to the temple. From the vertex, the channel enters the brain to re-emerge at the nape of the neck. From here, it flows down the occiput and all the way down the back. From the lumbar area, it enters the kidney and bladder. Another branch from the occiput runs down the back along the medial aspect of the scapula, down the back to gluteus and the popliteal fossa. Here it meets the previous branch and runs along the posterior aspect of the leg to end at the lateral apsect of the 5th toe where it links with the Kidney channel.

TENDINO MUSCULAR MERIDIAN: BL-67 to SI-18

DIVERGENT CHANNEL (DISTINCT MERIDIAN): BL-40, KI-10 to BL-10

TRANSVERSE LUO CHANNEL: BL-58 to KI-3

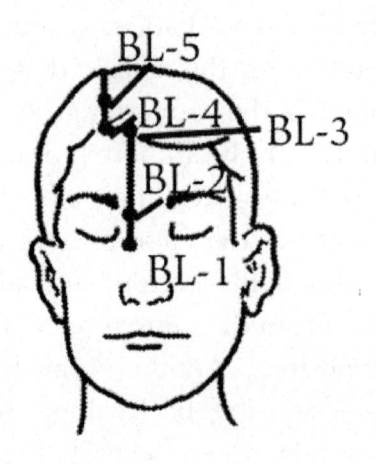

BL-1: *Jingming* (Eyes Bright)

0.1 cun superior to the inner canthus, in the medial palpebral ligament and in its deep position in the rectus medialis bulbi. Outside corner of the eye.

- Origin Point of the Bladder
- Intersection Point of the Small Intestine
- Intersection Point of the Stomach
- Entry Point

This point is very dangerous with even a light strike causing nausea followed by a loss of energy. If struck hard it may stop the natural flow of energy within the system and cause death.

This point stimulates the *Wei Qi*, or protective *Qi*. If attacked, the immune system is often damaged.

Activation angle: 90°

BL-2: *Zanzhu* (Gathered Bamboo / Drilling Bamboo)

In the Supraorbital notch at the medial end of the eyebrow, in the frontalis and corrugator supercillii muscles.

Another extremely dangerous point!

It can cause extreme draining of energy from the body.

Physically, it can injure the eye. A light strike can cause headaches to persist.

If struck upward, knock out and even death may result.

Activation angle: 15°

BL-3: *Meichong* (Eyebrow's Pouring)

Directly above the medial end of the eyebrow, 0.5 cun within the anterior hairline, between GV-24, and BL-4.

This point attacks the brain and can lead to knock out or death from a broken neck. This point is located above an area of the cerebrum which controls numerous functions within the body.

Energetically, this point drains energy from the body.

Activation angle: 15°

BL-4: *Quchai* (Discrepancy)

1.5 cun lateral to GV-24, at the junction of the medial third and the lateral two thirds of the distance between GV-24 and ST-8, within the natural hairline.

This point also attacks the brain and can lead to neurological shutdown.

This point is easily struck along with BL-3 simultaneously with the same blow.

This point is, however, fairly well protected.

Activation angle: 15°

BL-5: *Wuchu* (Five Places)

1.5 cun lateral to GV-23, directly above BL-4, 1 cun within the natural hairline.

This point needs less force to be effective than the preceding point. It causes localized pain with low power strikes. More powerful strikes can drain energy down through the body leading to nausea. Even harder strikes have been known to produce knock out.

Activation angle: 15°

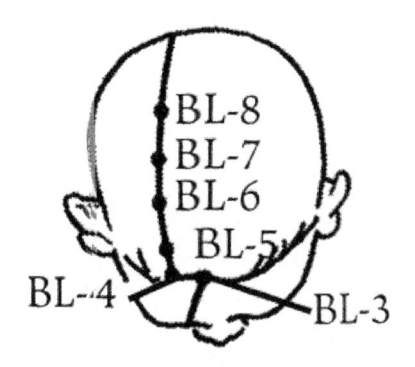

BL-6: *Chengguang* (Support Light)

1.5 cun posterior to BL-5, 1.5 cun lateral to the GV, 2.5 cun above the natural hairline.

This point can easily drain the energy.

With its location over the frontal fontanel, it has the capability of damaging the skull if struck hard.

Activation angle: 15°

BL-7: *Tongtian* (Reaching Heaven /Penetrating Heaven)

Draw a line approximately from the rear of the ear up to 1.5 cun from the middle line of the skull. Or 1.5 cun posterior to BL-6. 1.5 cun posterior to BL-6, 1.5 cun lateral to the GV. 4 cun with the hair line. The point is in the Galea aponeurotica, 1 cun anterior to GV-20.

Even a medium power strike can do damage to the brain causing confusion.

Activation angle: 15°

BL-8: *Luoque* (Decline)

On the top of the head, 1.5 cun posterior to BL-7, 1.5 cun lateral to the GV, 5.5 cun with in the hairline.

Localized pain is common. It can also cause a draining of energy possibly leading to knock out.

Activation angle: 15°

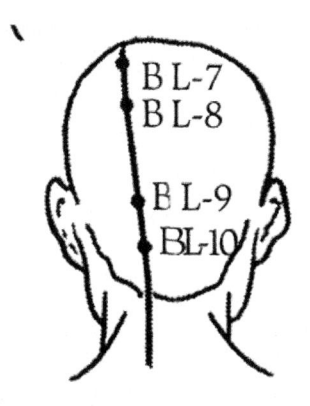

BL-9: *Yuzhen* (Jade Pillow)

1.3 cun lateral to GV-17, on the lateral side of the superior border of the external occipital protuberance.

This point is comparable to GB-19. It is also capable of draining the energy from the chest leading to nausea and possible cardiac arrest if the strike is hard enough.

Activation angle: 45°

BL-10: *Tianzhu* (Heavenly Pillar)

1.3 cun lateral to GV-15, within the posterior hairline on the lateral side of the trapezium in the origin of the trapezium and in its deep position in the semispinalis capitis muscle.

- Window of the Sky Point

Warning! Do not play around with this point!

This is an extremely dangerous point!

It can easily produce knockout with medium power strikes. Struck harder and respiration can be impaired due to the spinal vertebrae being attacked and their control of respiration.

This point is often paired with strikes to ST-9 and CV-17 for disastrous results. The combination of these points can stop the flow of energy within the body and are likely unrecoverable.

With its location just below the Medulla Oblongata, it is the lowest portion of the brain stem where the nerve fibers cross. These fibers carry signals from the opposing sides of the body to the brain.

Activation angle: 90°

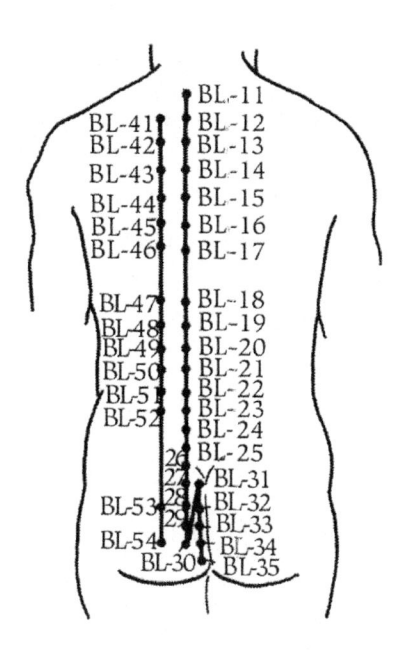

BL-11: *Dashu* (Big Shuttle)

1.5 cun lateral to the lower border (Big Shuttle) of the spinous process of the 1st thoracic vertebra, about 2 finger breadths from the GV. Superficially this point is located in the Trapezius, Rhomboid, poster superior Serratus muscles, and in its deep position in the Longissimus muscle.

- Origin Point of the Bladder
- Intersection Point of the Small Intestine
- Intersection Point of the Stomach
- Meeting-Hui Point of the bones

- Four Seas Point: Sea of Blood

This is also a deadly point!

This point affects the bones and kidneys. It can cause immediate nausea and massive energy drainage. It is often combined with ST-37 and ST-39 for lethal results.

Activation angle: 45°

BL-12: *Fengmen* (Winds Door)

1.5 cun lateral to the lower border of the spinous process of the 2nd thoracic vertebra. In the Trapezius, Rhomboid and posterior superior Serratus and in the deep position the Longissimus Innervation: Superficially, the medial cutaneous branches of the posterior rami of the 2nd and 3rd Thoracic nerves, deeper, their lateral cutaneous branches.

- Intersection Point of the Governing Vessel
- Origin Point of the Bladder

This point can easily impair energy circulation. It can also expose the spine to attack.

Activation angle: 45°

BL-13: *Feishu* (Lungs Hollow)

1.5 cun lateral to the lower border of the 3rd thoracic vertebra.

- Associated Point of the Lungs

This is the associated point for the lungs. It can also affect the kidneys.

The flow of *Wei Qi* is greatly affected by a strike to this point.

Activation angle: 45°

BL-14: *Jueyinshu* (Absolute Yin Hollow)

1.5 cun lateral to the lower border of the spinous process of the 4th thoracic vertebra. In the Trapezius and Rhomboid muscles and deeper, in the Longissimus muscle.

- Associated Point of the Pericardium

This point is connected with the Pericardium meridian. It can affect the Shen and the mind's communications. In addition, the Kidney's Jing is also affected by strikes to this point.

Activation angle: 45°

BL-15: *Xinshu* (Heart's Hollow)

1.5 cun lateral to the lower end of the 5th thoracic vertebra. In the Trapezius and Rhomboid muscles and deeper, in the Longissimus muscle.

- Associated Point of the Heart

This point is capable of damaging the heart and can lead to cardiac arrest. The "seat of power" is also vulnerable via the lungs and diaphragm.

Activation angle: 45°

BL-16: *Dashu* (Governing Hollow)

1.5 cun lateral to the lower border of the spinous process of the 6th thoracic vertebra. In the trapezium, latissimus dorsi and Longissimus muscles.

Energy will often drain at a later time and not always immediately after being struck.

Activation angle: 45°

BL-17: *Geshu* (Diaphragm's Hollow)

1.5 cun lateral to the lower border of the spinous process of the 7th thoracic vertebra. At the inferior margin of the trapezium, and in the latissimus dorsi and Longissimus muscles.

- Regulates the Spleen and Stomach
- Meeting-Hui Point of the Blood

Struck downwards, the body will be drained of energy; struck upwards, the throat is impaired.

Activation angle: 45°

BL-18: *Ganshu* (Liver's Hollow)

1.5 cun lateral to the lower border of the spinous process of the 9th thoracic vertebra. In the latissimus dorsi muscle, and between the Longissimus and iliocostalis muscles.

- Associated Point of the Liver
- Regulates the Spleen and Stomach

Struck accurately, this point may cause extreme nausea and can even impair the vision.

This point is an Associated Point for the liver. It has the capacity also of injuring the gall bladder. Injury to the liver, or even perceived injury by the brain, often leads to knock out.

Activation angle: 90°

BL-19: *Danshu* (Gall Bladder's Hollow)

1.5 cun lateral to the lower border of the spinous process of the 10th thoracic vertebra. In the latissimus dorsi muscle, between the ilocostalis and Longissimus muscles.

- Associated Point of the Gall Bladder

Comparable to the BL-17 point.

It is often employed in combination with GB-25 and LV-14.

Activation angle: 90°

BL-20: *Pishu* (Spleen Hollow)

1.5 cun lateral to the lower border of the spinous process of the 11th thoracic vertebra. In the latissimus dorsi muscle, between the Longissimus and iliocostalis muscles.

- Associated Point of the Spleen
- Regulates the Spleen and Stomach

This point may cause vomiting when struck due to its attack on the stomach, spleen, liver, and gall bladder.

It can greatly disrupt the circulation of energy within the body.

Activation angle: 90°

BL-21: *Weishu* (Stomach's Hollow)

1.5 cun lateral to the lower border of the spinous process of the 12th thoracic vertebra. In the lumbodorsal fascia, between the Longissimus and iliocostalis muscles.

- Associated Point of the Stomach
- Regulates the Spleen and Stomach

Can cause extreme nausea and weakness. Also capable of injuring the liver.

Activation angle: 90°

BL-22: *Sanjiaoshu* (Triple Burner's Hollow)

1.5 cun lateral to the lower border of the spinous process of the 1st lumbar vertebra. In the lumbodorsal fascia, between the Longissimus and iliocostalis muscles.

- Associated Point of the Triple Burner
- Regulates the Spleen and Stomach

This point affects the Water of the body and the Triple Heater, which controls the flow of energy throughout the body.

Activation angle: 90°

BL-23: *Shenshu* (Kidney's Hollow)

1.5 cun lateral to the lower border of the spinous process of the 2nd lumbar vertebra. In the lumbodorsal fascia, between the longissimus and iliocostalis muscles.

- Associated Point of the Kidney
- Regulates the Spleen and Stomach

This is the Shu Point of the kidneys. So great kidney damage is done. Not as much as a strike to GB 25, but enough to cause considerable kidney failure or blood in the urine.

Activation angle: 90°

BL-24: *Qihaishu* (Sea of Qi Hollow)

1.5 cun lateral to the lower border of the spinous process of the 3rd lumbar vertebra. In the lumbodorsal fascia, between the longissimus and iliocostalis muscles.

This point drains the legs and back.

Activation angle: 90°

BL-25: *Dachangshu* (Colon's Hollow)

1.5 cun lateral to the lower border of the spinous process of the 4th lumbar vertebra. In the lumbodorsal fascia, between the longissimus and iliocostalis muscles.

- Associated Point of the Large Intestine
- Regulates the Spleen and Stomach

Associated Point for the Large Intestine. Strikes often lead to nausea and great localized pain. It can also drain the Lower Burner.

Activation angle: 90°

BL-26: *Guanyuanshu* (Hinge at the Source)

1.5 cun lateral to the lower border of the spinous process of the 5th lumbar vertebra. In the sacrospinalis muscle.

This point is the Associated Point for the Vital Essence. It is connected with the Penetrating Vessel.

Striking this point leads to massive energy drainage.

Activation angle: 90°

BL-27: *Xiaochangshu* (Small Intestine's Hollow)

At the level of the 1st posterior sacral foramen, 1.5 cun lateral to the GV. Between the origins of the sacrospinalis and gluteus maximus muscle.

- Associated Point of the Small Intestine
- Regulates the Spleen and Stomach

Can cause vomiting and nausea.

Activation angle: 90°

BL-28: *Pangguangshu* (Bladder's Hollow)

At the level of the 2nd posterior sacral foramen, 1.5 cun lateral to the GV, in the depression between the medial border of the posterior superior iliac spine and the sacrum. The point is between the origins of the sacrospinalis and gluteus maximus muscles.

- Associated Point of the Bladder
- Regulates the Spleen and Stomach

Can cause energy drainage and even knock out with a hard strike.

Activation angle: 90°

BL-29: *Zhonglushu* (Mid Spine Hollow)

At the level of the 3rd posterior sacral foramen, 1.5 cun lateral to the GV, between the origins of the sacrospinalis and gluteus maximum muscles.

Strikes can drain the legs and disrupt the body.

Activation angle: 90°

BL-30: *Baihuanshu* (White Circle's Hollow)

At the level of the fourth sacral foramen, 1.5 cun lateral to the GV. In the gluteus maximus muscle and the inferior, medial margin of the sacrotuberous ligament.

Can physically damage the coccyx bone.

Activation angle: 90°

BL-31: *Shangliao* (Upper Hole)

The points, BL-31 To BL-34 are collectively called *Baliao* meaning, "Eight Seams."

In the 1st sacral foramen, roughly midway between the posterior superior iliac spine and the GV. In the sacrospinalis and the origin of the gluteus maximus muscle.

Because of its proximity to the spine, spinal damage is feasible from a hard blow.

Activation angle: 90°

BL-32: *Ciliao* (Second Bone) (Part of *Baliao*)

In the 2nd posterior sacral foramen, about mid-way between the lower border of the posterior superior iliac spike and the GV. In the sacrospinalis and the origin of the gluteus maximus muscle.

Striking this point can weaken the legs and cause spasm in the muscles leading to temporary paralysis.

Activation angle: 90°

BL-33: *Zhongliao* (Middle Hole, Part of *Baliao*)

In the 3rd posterior sacral foramen, between BL-29 and the GV. In the sacrospinalis and the origin of the gluteus maximus muscle.

Comparable to the previous point. This point may also injure the Lower Heater.

Activation angle: 90°

BL-34: *Xialiao* (Lower Hole) (Part of *Baliao*)

In the 4th posterior sacral foramen, between BL-30 and the GV. In the sacrospinalis and the origin of the gluteus maximus muscle.

Comparable to the previous point.

BL-35: *Huiyang* (Meeting of *Yang*)

0.5 cun lateral to the Lip of the coccyx.

Physical damage to the coccyx bone is likely. If broken, knock out may occur due to the great pain.

Energetically, this point affects the Upper Heavenly Flow of *Qi*.

Activation angle: 45°

BL-36: *Chengfu* (Receive Support)

In the middle of the transverse gluteal fold below the buttock. At the inferior margin of the gluteus maximus muscle.

Striking this point often sends massive amounts of *Yang Qi* into the head leading to knock out if struck hard enough.

It is very difficult to reach however.

Activation angle: 45°

BL-37: *Yinmen* (Door of Abundance)

6 cun below BL-36, on the line joining BL-36 to BL-40, in the semitendinous muscle.

There is little damage done from striking.

Activation angle: 90°

BL-38: *Fuxi* (Floating Xi)

1 cun above BL-39, on the medial side of the tendon of biceps femoris. The point is located with the knee slightly flexed.

This point can easily damage the knee and leg. It is often paired with KI-10.

Activation angle: 45°

BL-39: *Weiyang* (Commanding Yang)

When the person is prone, this point can be found 1 cun lateral to BL-40, on the medial border of the tendon of biceps femoris in the popliteal fossa.

- Lower Uniting-He Point of the Triple Burner
- Uniting-He Point of the Triple Burner

This point can damage the bladder easily as well as the knee.

Attacking the surrounding kidney points along with KI-10 can cause the kidneys to fail!

Activation angle: 45°

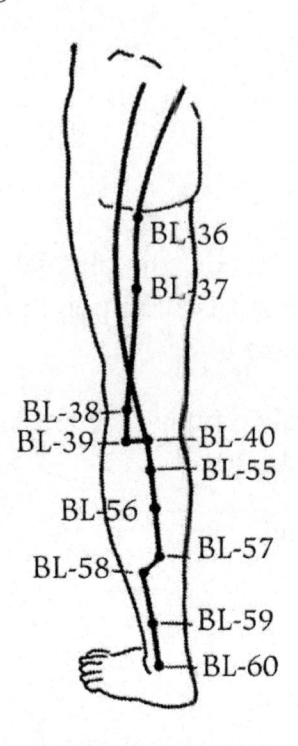

BL-40: *Weizhong* (Commanding Middle)

Midpoint of the transverse crease of the popliteal fossa, in the fascia of the popliteal fossa between the tendons of biceps femoris and semitendinous. Locate the point in the prone position with the knee flexed.

- Lower Uniting-He Point of the Bladder
- Earth Point

- Uniting-He Point of the Bladder
- Command Point of the back
- One of 36 Vital Points Listed in the Bubishi

This is an earth point and also a he point. It can cause spasm in the tendons.

Knock out has been known to occur with this point due to a sudden rush of energy into the head.

Activation angle: 45°

BL-41: *Fufen* (Appended Part)

3 cun lateral to the lower border of the spinous process of the 2nd thoracic vertebra. This is about four finger breadths (of patient) lateral to the midline of the spine.

- Origin Point of the Bladder
- Intersection Point of the Small Intestine

With its close proximity to BL-12, both can be easily struck together, seriously draining the energy from the body.

Activation angle: 45°

BL-42: *Pohu* (Soul's Household)

3 cun lateral to the lower border of the spinous process of the 3rd thoracic vertebra.

Comparable to the previous point.

It does have the ability to drain the lungs and upper body more. It also lies in proximity to the heart and can affect it and can lead to cardiac arrest if struck hard enough.

Activation angle: 90°

BL-43: *Gaohuangshu* (Vital's Hollow)

3 cun lateral to the lower border of the spinous process of the 4th thoracic vertebra. At the end of the medial border of the spine of the scapula, in the trapezium and rhomboid muscles, in the deep position the iliocostalis muscle.

- One of 36 Vital Points Listed in the Bubishi

This is the Associated Point of the Vital Center of the body. It has the ability to drain energy from the lungs and slow down the entire energetic system leading to overall weakness and possible loss of consciousness.

Activation angle: 90°

BL-44: *Shentang* (Spirit's Hall)

3 cun lateral to the lower border of the spinous process of the 5th thoracic vertebra.

This point can drain the lungs.

Activation angle: 90°

BL-45: *Yixi* (Surprise)

3 cun lateral to the spinous process of the 6th thoracic vertebra.

Drainage point, especially when combined with HT-5, LU-5, or LU-8.

Activation angle: 90°

BL-46: *Geguan* (Diaphragm's Hinge)

3 cun lateral to the lower border of the 7th thoracic vertebra, approximately at the level of the inferior angle of the scapula.

This point can affect the heart and lungs and do great damage to the energetic system due to its attack to the diaphragm. It can also affect the muscular system as well.

Activation angle: 90°

BL-47: *Hunmen* (Soul's Door)

3 cun lateral to lower border of the spinous process of the 9th thoracic vertebra.

This point is capable of doing great harm to the lungs.

Activation angle: 90°

BL-48: *Yanggang* (Yang's Parameter)

3 cun lateral to the lower border of the spinous process of the 10th thoracic vertebra.

This point can obstruct the *Yang Qi* and injure the lungs, impairing respiration.

Activation angle: 90°

BL-49: *Yishe* (Will's Residence)

3 cun lateral to the lower border of the spinous process of the 11th thoracic vertebra.

Comparable to the previous point. In addition, it can affect the mind and lead to confusion.

Activation angle: 90°

BL-50: *Weicang* (Stomach's Storehouse)

3 cun lateral to the lower border of the spinous process of the 12th thoracic vertebra.

Attacks the stomach. It can cause *Yang* energy to rise.

Activation angle: 90°

BL-51: *Huangmen* (Vitals' Door)

3 cun lateral to the lower border of the spinous process of the 1st lumbar vertebra.

- One of 36 Vital Points Listed in the Bubishi

If employed with BL-22, it can cause cardiac arrest.

Activation angle: 90°

BL-52: *Zhishi* (Will's Dwelling)

3 cun lateral to the lower border of the spinous process of the 2nd lumbar vertebra. In the latissimus dorsi and iliocostalis muscles.

This point often drains the leg on the opposing side of the body. It can destroy the will to fight, especially if coupled with ST-12.

Activation angle: 45°

BL-53: *Baohuang* (Placenta and Vitals)

3 cun lateral to the lower border of the spinous process of the 2nd sacral vertebra, level with BL-32.

Comparable to BL-28.

Activation angle: 90°

BL-54: *Zhibian* (Order's Edge)

Directly below BL-53. Located 3 cun lateral to the spinous process of the 4th sacral vertebra. In the gluteus maximus muscle and the inferior margin of the piriformis muscle.

- Destructive Point

This point is often struck together with BL-30, 34, and 54, causing massive drainage of energy.

Activation angle: 90°

BL-55: *Heyang* (Confluence of Yang)

2 cun directly below BL-40, between the medial and lateral heads of the gastrocnemius, on the line that joins BL-40, to BL-57.

This point can easily injure the legs and drain them of energy. It can also cause *Yang Qi* to rise into the brain leading to knock out.

Activation angle: 90°

BL-56: *Chengjin* (Support Sinews)

In the center of the belly of the gastrocnemius, midway between BL-55 and BL-57.

This point is often used to escape grappling holds or can be struck with a kick, injuring the leg.

Activation angle: 90°

BL-57: *Chengshan* (Support Mountain)

If person lies prone, this point can be found by stretching the foot as if standing on tip-toe. This reveals a triangular shaped hollow in the middle of the calf, about midway between the point BL-40 and the heel. The point is at the top of this triangle, at the lower border of the separation of the two bellies of the gastrocnemius muscle.

This point can cause the body to collapse on the leg. It causes immediate localized pain when pressed or struck. Neural shock is also common.

Activation angle: 90°

BL-58: *Feiyang* (Soaring Flying High)

7 cun directly above BL-60, on the posterior border of the fibula, approximately 1 cun inferior and lateral to BL-57. In the gastrocnemius and soleus muscles.

- Connecting-luo Point of the Kidney

This point can shock the system and cause the person to "freeze" in their movements. This point upset the balance of *Yin* and *Yang*.

Activation angle: 90°

BL-59: *Fuyang* (Tarsal Yang)

3 cun directly above BL-60, on the lateral aspect of the gastrocnemius muscle.

- Origin Point of the Bladder
- Intersection Point of the Yang Motility vessel
- Cleft-xi Point

This is a Xie-cleft point, or accumulation point.

It can also affect the head and lead to headaches.

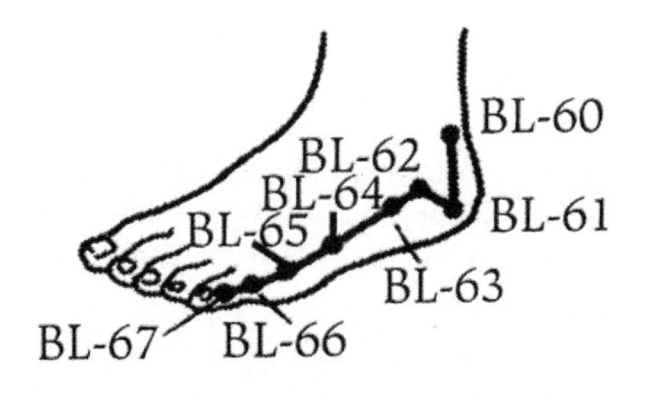

Activation angle: 90°

BL-60: *Kunlun* (Kunlun Mountain)

In the depression midway between the lateral malleolus and the Achilles tendon, in the peroneus brevis muscle.

- Fire Point
- River-jing Point

This point can easily weaken the upper body.

It is a fire and jing point, which means it normally balances the Fire and Water of the body. When struck the opposite occurs, and that balance is upset. It can cause massive energy drainage.

Activation angle: 90°

BL-61: *Pushen* (Serve and Consult)

Posterior and inferior to the external malleus, directly below BL-60, in the depression of the calcaneum at the junction of the red and white skin.

- Origin Point of the Bladder
- Intersection Point of the Yang Motility vessel

This point drains energy and can lead to a great deal of localized pain.

Activation angle: 45°

BL-62: *Shenmai* (Extending/Expressing Vessel)

In the depression at the inferior margin of the lateral malleolus of the ankle.

- Origin Point of the Bladder
- Intersection Point of the Yang Motility vessel
- Master Point of the Yang Motility vessel
- Coupled Point with Extraordinary Meridian of the Governing Vessel
- Associated with an Extraordinary Vessel of the Yang Motility vessel
- One of 36 Vital Points Listed in the Bubishi

This point can damage the tendons and nerves as well as drain energy.

Activation angle: 45°

BL-63: *Jinmen* (Golden Door)

Anterior and inferior to BL-62, in the depression lateral to the cuboid bone.

- Origin Point of the Bladder
- Intersection Point of the Yang Linking Vessel
- Cleft-xi Point

This is a Xie-cleft point, or accumulation point.

Although it affects the *Wei Qi* of the body, it is difficult to get much of a reaction at this point.

Activation angle: 45°

BL-64: *Jinggu* (Capital Bone)

On the lateral side of the dorsum of the foot, below the tuberosity of the 5th metatarsal bone, at the junction of the red and white skin, at the inferior margin of the lateral abductor digiti minimi pedis.

- Source Point

This is a Source Point and can cause the kidney damage if struck.

Activation angle: 45°

BL-65: *Shugu* (Restraining Bone)

On the lateral side of the dorsum of the foot, posterior and inferior to the head of the 5th metatarsal bone, at the junction of the red and white skin.

- Wood Point
- Stream-shu Point
- Sedation Point

This is a Wood and Associated Point.

Strikes may cause confusion and blurred vision. The *Wei Qi* is often impaired.

Activation angle: 45°

BL-66: *Zutonggu* (Connecting Valley of the Foot)

In the depression anterior and inferior to the 5th metatarsal phalangeal joint.

- Spring-ying Point
- Water Point
- Horary Point

This is a Water and spring, or stream point.

It is comparable to the previous point.

Activation angle: 45°

BL-67: *Zhiyin* (End of *Yin*)

On the lateral side of the little toe, about 0.1 cun posterior to the lateral corner of the toenail.

- Well-jing Point
- Metal Point
- Tonification Point
- Exit Point

This is a Metal, cheng, and root point of 'tai yang' and extra meridians.

It can injure the tendons and muscles of the whole body. Strikes can cause confusion. Energetically, it often damages the kidneys.

Activation angle: 15°

Chapter 13

The Conception Vessel

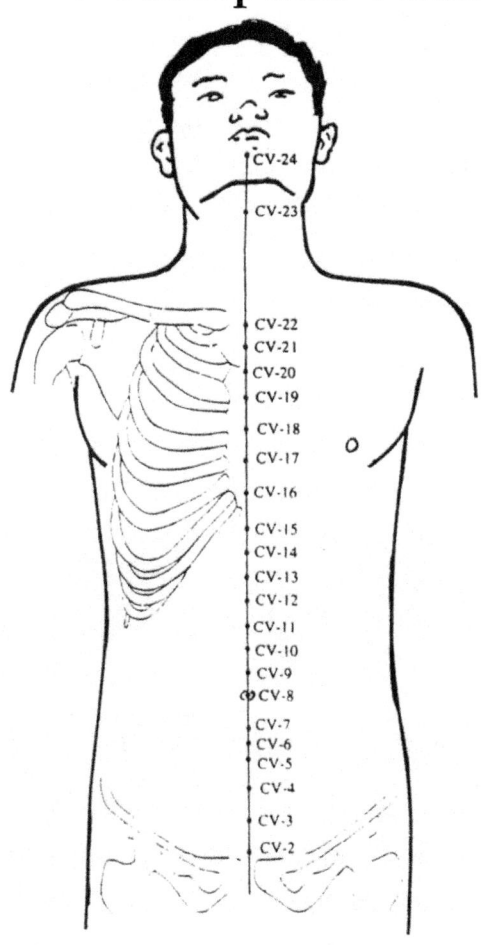

Conception Vessel Meridian Overview	
Alternative Name(s)	Directing Vessel
Chinese Name	*Ren Mai*
Paired Meridian(s)	Yin Heel Vessel
Master Point	LU-7
Coupled Point	KI-6
Xi-Cleft Point	N/A
Connecting Point	CV-15
Intersection Point(s)	ST-1, GV-28

Areas of effect

Face, thorax, abdomen, genitals, throat, chest, lungs, endocrine, urinary and digestive systems

Functions

- "Sea of Yin" influences the yin, essence and fluids.
- Regulates female cycles, menstruation (irregular, leucorrhea), and reproduction.

- Effects male genitalia, hernia, sexual desire, and impotence.

- Gastrointestinal issues, digestion.

MAIN CHANNEL PATHWAY

Originates at ming men and passes through the uterus and connects with CV-1. Then it follows the Conception Vessel up to CV-24. Along the path it connects internally with the SP, LV and KI meridians. At CV-24 a second branch rises upwards and encircles the mouth and then rises to the eyes at ST-1. A separate branch originates in the pelvic cavity and rises up along the back.

CONNECTING CHANNEL PATHWAY
This channel starts at the tip of the xyphoid process from the point Jiuwei CV-15 and spreads over the abdomen.

INTERSECTIONS:
Receives energy from Liver at CV-2; energy from three yin of legs at CV-3; energy from Kidney at CV-7; energy from Spleen and Liver at CV-10; energy from five Zang at CV-17.

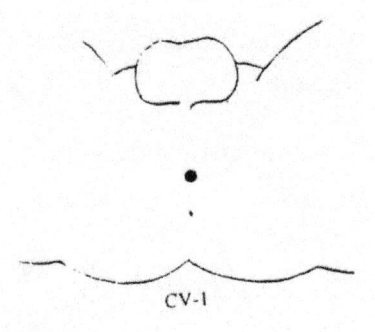

CV-1: *Huiyin* (Perineum)

In the center of the perineum. Midway between the anus and the scrotum in men and midway between the anus and commissura labiorum in females. *Hui* means "crossing" and *Yin* here is referring to the genitalia. The point is located in the space between the genitalia and the anus.

- Origin Point of the Conception Vessel
- Intersection Point of the Penetrating Vessel
- Associated with an Extraordinary Vessel of the (CV, GV, and Penetrating Vessel)
- One of 36 Vital Points Listed in the Bubishi

This is an extremely dangerous point that may result in death or coma when struck. It is difficult to get to unless the person is either in a deep horse stance or is kicking.

Activation angle: 90°

CV-2: *Qugu* (Crooked Bone)

On the mid-line of the abdomen, just above the symphysis pubis. 5 cun below the umbilicus, at the superior aspect of the symphysis pubic.

- Origin Point of the Conception Vessel
- Intersection Point of the Kidney

This point may cause knock out if struck with medium power. Death may occur if struck harder.

Activation angle: 90°

CV-3: *Zhongji* (Middle Summit or Central Pole)

On the anterior mid-line, 4 cun below the umbilicus, 1 cun above the upper border of the symphysis pubis. *Zhong* means "center" and *Ji* means "exactly." The point is exactly at the center of the body.

- Origin Point of the Conception Vessel
- Intersection Point of the Spleen

- Intersection Point of the Yang Linking Vessel

- Alarm Point of the Bladder

A strike can be very damaging to the Spleen, Kidney, and the Liver with great energetic disruption. This can be fatal.

Activation angle: 90°

CV-4: *Guanyuan* (Hinge at the Source or Gate Origin)

On the midline of the abdomen, 3 cun below the umbilicus.

- Origin Point of the Conception Vessel

- Intersection Point of the Spleen

- Intersection Point of the Pericardium

- Intersection Point of the Yin Linking Vessel

- Alarm Point of the Small Intestine

- Associated with an Extraordinary Vessel of the Conception Vessel

- One of 36 Vital Points Listed in the Bubishi

This point is extremely dangerous when struck. It is located directly underneath the *tantien*, the energy center of the body approximately three inches below the navel.

A hard blow may impair the flow of energy through the entire body and cause system failure. This can prove to be fatal. Strike downwards often drains the energy from the body; struck upwards can increase the blood pressure and lead to dizziness; struck perpendicularly, it can impair the flow of energy.

Activation angle: 90°

CV-5: *Shimen* (Stone Door)

On the midline of the abdomen, 2 cun below the umbilicus.

- Alarm Point of the Triple Burner

This point is often referred to as the *tantien* point, or *Mingmen*. Acupuncture teaches that needling this point may decrease life span; striking it will likely have the same result!

I am aware of a person who was struck here in a downwards direction and went immediately into shock. After being rushed into surgery and several feet of their intestines removed, they continued to suffer and required numerous follow-up operations. After almost a year of these, their physical condition had diminished so greatly, they were a pale reflection of their former self. It is not likely that their health will ever return to its former quality.

The points in this region should be avoided as much as possible, unless a fatality is the intended result. They are extremely dangerous!

Activation angle: 90°

CV-6: *Qihai* (Sea of QI)

On the mid-line of the abdomen, 1.5 cun below the umbilicus or half way between CV-7 and CV-5.

This point could be very easily fatal and unrecoverable. Strikes upset the entire energetic system. Effects of this energetic disruption may even manifest days later. It is a comparable to a clock whose batteries are running down and it continues to slow until it eventually stops.

If struck harder, death may result instantly. The Kidneys will be affected immediately, as well as the heart.

Activation angle: 90°

CV-7: *Yinjiao* (Yin's Junction)

On the mid-line of the abdomen, 1 cun below the umbilicus.

- Origin Point of the Conception Vessel
- Intersection Point of the Penetrating Vessel
- Four Seas Point: Sea of Qi

This point is slightly less dangerous than the previous six points, but is still to be avoided for general practice nonetheless.

Direct stimulation may produce knock out and harder strikes may be fatal due to kidney failure.

Activation angle: 90°

CV-8: *Qizhong* (Middle of Navel)

In the middle of the umbilicus.

This point is not very well protected by the abdominal muscles. The centerline is often very exposed, even on muscular people.

This point may injure the spleen and the stomach directly due to its location.

Energetically, energy may rush into the head, leading to knock out or even death if the strike is severe enough. It can disperse the Yang *Qi*.

Activation angle: 90°

CV-9: *Shuifen* (Division Of Water)

On the mid-line of the abdomen, 1 cun above the umbilicus.

This point can energetically disrupt the lungs, spleen, and the kidneys, if you can overcome the physical protection afforded this point.

Activation angle: 90°

CV-10: *Xiawan* (Lower Cavity)

On the midline of the abdomen, 2 cun above the umbilicus.

- Origin Point of the Conception Vessel
- Intersection Point of the Spleen

Similar to CV-12 and CV-13, this point will hinder the body's ability to produce energy, shortening the life-span. This could occur even within days of a hard strike.

Activation angle: 90°

CV-11: *Jianli* (Establish Measure)

On the midline of the abdomen, 3 cun above the umbilicus.

This point is fairly well protected by surrounding tissue. If the strike is made will the muscles are relaxed, however, it is not too difficult to attack.

This point can drain the body of energy and lead to knock out.

Activation angle: 90°

CV-12: *Zhongwan* (Middle Cavity)

On the mid-line of the abdomen, 4 cun above the umbilicus. *Zhong* means "middle" and *Wan* means "stomach." The point lies in the middle of the stomach.

- Origin Point of the Conception Vessel

- Alarm Point of the Stomach
- Downbears Qi
- Meeting-Hui Point of the Bowels

This point is comparable to CV-10. In addition, it may cause vomiting and diarrhea to occur after being struck hard.

This point is the Alarm Point for the stomach. It is a special meeting point of the *Yang*, or hollow, organs. It is also the meeting point of the middle and triple heaters.

With all of its energetic interconnections, it will cause disharmony between the *Yin* and the *Yang*.

Activation angle: 90°

CV-13: *Shangwan* (Upper Cavity)

On the mid-line of the abdomen, 5 cun above the umbilicus.

- Origin Point of the Conception Vessel

This point is comparable to CV-10 and CV-12. In addition, it may affect the heart and the lungs. It can drain energy leading to overall weakness of the body.

Activation angle: 90°

CV-14: *Juque* (Great Palace or Shrine)

On the mid-line of the abdomen, 6 cun above the umbilicus or 1 cun below the xiphoid process of the sternum.

- Alarm Point of the Heart

This is an extremely dangerous point and may prove fatal if struck hard.

This point is the Alarm Point for the heart and may cause cardiac arrest if struck.

Activation angle: 90°

CV-15: *Jiuwei* (Wild Pigeon's Tail)

0.5 cun below the xiphoid process of the sternum or 7 cun above the umbilicus. Locate the point in supine position with the arms uplifted.

- Connecting-luo Point of the Governing Vessel
- Associated with an Extraordinary Vessel of the Conception Vessel

- One of 36 Vital Points Listed in the Bubishi

This point is comparable (but slightly less dangerous) to CV-14 and can also cause cardiac arrest.

Activation angle: 90°

CV-16: *Zhongting* (Middle Hall or Courtyard)

On the middle of the sternum, level with the 5th intercostal space or 1.6 cun below CV-17.

This point is located between the xiphoid process and the sternum. It is exposed even on muscular people, making it very vulnerable to attack.

It is capable of causing nausea and vomiting and even knock out with medium power blows. Harder blows may prove fatal.

Activation angle: 90°

CV-17: *Shangzong* or *Tanzhong* (Penetrating Odour)

- On the mid-line of the sternum, between the nipples, level with the 4th intercostal space. *Tan* means "exposure" and *Zhong* means "middle."

- Origin Point of the Conception Vessel
- Intersection Point of the Spleen
- Intersection Point of the Kidney
- Alarm Point of the Pericardium
- Downbears Qi
- Meeting-Hui Point of the Qi

The Point is located at the exposed middle part of the chest called *Tanzhong* in ancient times.

This is an extremely dangerous point! This point can drain energy from the "seat of power," or the diaphragm.

Struck downward, can cause knock out or even death. Struck on younger people can prove fatal due to the fact that the sternum may be weaker. As one ages, the bones and cartilage of the chest solidify and become stronger, offering more protection.

This point is the Alarm Point for the pericardium, or protector of the heart. It is the meeting point for the Shao Yin, or sea of energy which meets with ST-9 and BL-10. It is also the meeting point of the upper and triple burner.

Its function is to regulate the flow of energy for the entire body and striking it impairs that function. It may also impair the balance between Water and Fire.

Activation angle: 15°

CV-18: *Yutang* (Jade Court)

On the mid-line of the sternum, level with the 3rd intercostal space, 1.6 cun above CV-17.

- Associated with an Extraordinary Vessel of the Conception Vessel
- One of 36 Vital Points Listed in the Bubishi

Although this point is fairly well protected by surrounding tissue, it can be dangerous if struck when the person is relaxed. A strong blow may also penetrate to the point.

Localized pain is common. Energy is drained as well, especially when the attack is very accurate to the point.

Activation angle: 15°

CV-19: *Zigong* (Purple Palace)

On the mid-line of the sternum, level with the 2nd intercostal space, 1.6 cun above CV-18.

This point is comparable to the previous one.

It is often struck with a single knuckle.

Activation angle: 15°

CV-20: *Huagai* (Lustrous Cover)

On the mid-line of the sternum, at the level of the 1st intercostal space or 1 cun below CV-21 which is much more dangerous.

- Intersection Point of the Bladder
- Origin Point of the Governing Vessel

Comparable to CV-19 in effect.

CV-21: *Xuanji* (North Star)

On the mid-line of the sternum, midway between CV-22 and CV-20, or midway between the articulations of the left and right rib with the sternum. *Xuan* here means "rotation" and *ji* means "axis." This is the name given to the 2nd and 3rd stars of the big dipper, opposite the *Zigong* star. This point is above *Zigong* point so is called *Xuanji*.

This point is less applicable to Martial Arts usage than nearby point CV-22.

Activation angle: 15°

CV-22: *Tiantu* (Heaven's Prominence)

In the depression 0.5 cun above the suprasternal notch, between the left and right sternocleidomastoid muscles. In it's deep position in the sternohyoid and sternothyroid muscles.

- Origin Point of the Conception Vessel
- Intersection Point of the Yin Linking Vessel
- Downbears Qi
- Window of the Sky Point
- Associated with an Extraordinary Vessel of the CV and Yin Linking Vessel.
- One of 36 Vital Points Listed in the Bubishi

This point is extremely dangerous! Striking it hard may lead to suffocation and death. Medium power will often impair mental activity.

This point is known to affect the lungs leading to violent coughing and a loss of breath.

Activation angle: 15°

CV-23: *Lianquan* (Modesty's Spring or Screen Spring)

Located above the Adam's apple, in the depression at the upper border of the hyoid bone. In the depression between the pharyngeal prominence and the lower margin of the hyoid bone.

- Origin Point of the Conception Vessel
- Intersection Point of the Yin Linking Vessel

This point is a special point related to the Shao Yin via the heart and kidney.

Struck hard, suffocation may occur and can lead to death. Struck upward can by-pass what little protection there is at this point and attack the trachea directly.

Activation angle: 90°

CV-24: *Chengjiang* (Contains Fluids or Receives Fluids)

In the depression in the center of the mentolabial groove. This is the depression below the middle of the lower lip between the orbicularis oris and mentalis muscle muscles.

- Origin Point of the Conception Vessel
- Origin Point of the Governing Vessel
- Intersection Point of the Small Intestine
- Intersection Point of the Triple Burner
- Associated with an Extraordinary Vessel of the Conception Vessel and Governing Vessel.
- One of 36 Vital Points Listed in the Bubishi

If struck from the outside with a single knuckle or pointed weapon, this point may produce nausea, knock out, or even death.

Activation angle: 90°

Chapter 14

The Governing Vessel

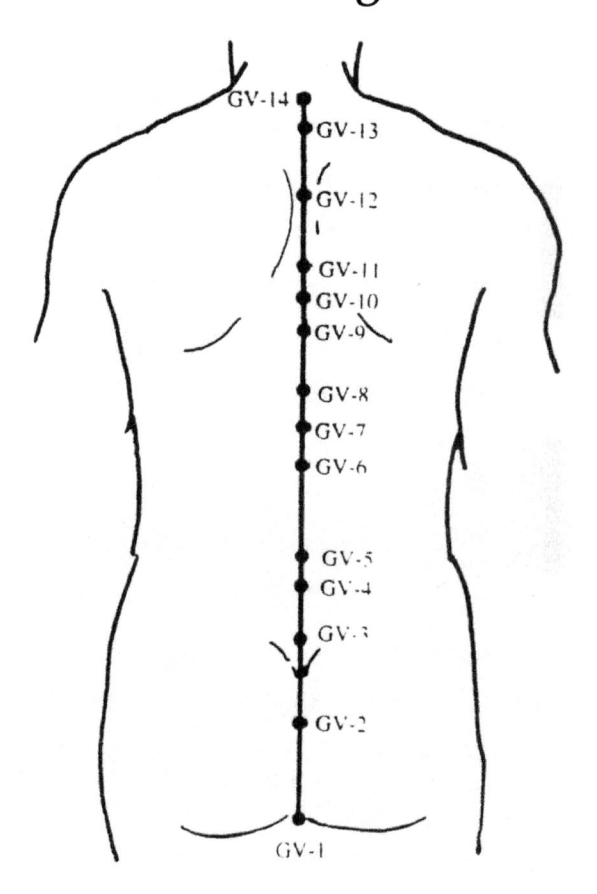

Governing Vessel Meridian Overview	
Alternative Name(s)	N/A
Chinese Name	*Du Mai*
Paired Meridian(s)	Yang Heel Vessel
Master Point	SI-3
Coupled Point	BL-62
Xi-Cleft Point	N/A
Connecting Point	GV-1
Intersection Point(s)	CV-1, BL-12

Areas of effect

Posterior midline especially spinal cord and brain, nervous and muscular systems.

Functions

- "Sea of Yang:" affects all of the yang meridians.

- Brain, marrow and/or spinal cord issues - pain, heaviness, stroke, psychological issues, etc.

- Other facial issues - headache, migraines, pain/swelling in the face/head.

MAIN CHANNEL PATHWAY
The Governing Vessel originates from the uterus (or deep inside the lower abdomen in men) and goes to the perineum where it emerges. It then ascends on the midline all the way up the back and neck to Fengfu GV-16 where it eners the brain. It then ascends tthte vertex and downs the front of the face to the upper lip.

CONNECTING CHANNEL PATHWAY
After separating from the point Changjiang GV-1, the Connecting channel flows upwards along both sides of the spine to the occiput from where it scatters over the top of the head. At the scapulae, a branch joins the Bladder channels and the upper spine.

GV-1: *Changqiang* (Long Strength)

Midway between the tip of the coccyx and the anus. *Chang* means "long" and *Qiang* means "strong." The spinal column is long and strong and the point is located at the lower end of the spinal column below the tail bone.

- Origin Point of the Governing Vessel
- Intersection Point of the Gall Bladder
- Connecting-luo Point of the Conception Vessel
- Stems counterflow
- Associated with an Extraordinary Vessel of the Governing Vessel
- One of 36 Vital Points Listed in the Bubishi

Striking the point straight up into the body can lead to a loss of consciousness and damage to the anus.

This point is the connecting point of the eight extraordinary vessels. Injury to this point could be fatal due to all of the energetic connections. It is also the Sea of Yang point.

Unfortunately, its location makes it a difficult point to attack!

Activation angle: 45°

GV-2: *Yaoshu* (Lower Back's Hollow)

In the hiatus of the sacrum.

This point will primarily injure the body physically and requires a very powerful strike to have any effect.

Activation angle: 45°

GV-3: *Yaoyangguan* (Lumbar Yang's Hinge)

Below the spinous process of the 4th lumbar vertebra, in the lumbodorsal fascia and the supraspinal and interspinal ligaments.

This point controls the energy flow to the Kidneys. As such, it can weaken the legs due to the support that the Kidneys provide to the legs.

This point is often paired with SP-19.

Activation angle: 90°

GV-4: *Mingmen* (Life's Door or Gate of Life)

Below the spinous process of the 2nd lumbar vertebra, in the lumbodorsal fascia and the supraspinal and interspinal ligaments.

- Stems counterflow

This point is extremely dangerous! Striking this point is known to affect the entire *Yang* system of the body and can injure the Kidneys.

Activation angle: 90°

GV-5: *Xuanshu* (Suspended Axis)

Below the spinous process of the 1st lumbar vertebra.

This point can affect breathing. In order to do this, however, the strike needs to be very accurate.

Activation angle: 90°

GV-6: *Jizhong* (Middle of Spine)

Ji here means "spine" and *Zhong* means "middle." The spine has a total of 21 vertebra. This Point is below the spinous process of the 11th vertebra and is therefore in the middle of the spine.

This point is very comparable to GV-5 in effect.

Activation angle: 90°

GV-7: *Zhongshu* (Middle Axis)

This point is below the spinous process of the 10th thoracic vertebra and is like a pivot in the middle of the spine. Zhong means middle and Shu means pivot.

Comparable to GV-6, but with slightly more possibility for lung damage. It is also capable of being more dangerous to the brain and can lead to knock out.

Activation angle: 90°

GV-8: *Jinsuo* (Sinew's Shrinking)

Below the spinous process of the 9th thoracic vertebra.

Comparable to GV-7, but even more dangerous to the lungs. It may also affect the vision when struck really hard.

Activation angle: 90°

GV-9: *Zhiyang* (Reaching Yang)

Below the spinous process of the 7th thoracic vertebra, in the supraspinal and interspinal ligaments.

- Nourishes the Blood

This point can impair the lungs and lead to coughing. Energetically, it will drain the energy, especially in the liver and gall bladder.

Struck hard enough it may injure the spinal column.

Activation angle: 90°

GV-10: *Lingtai* (Spirit's Platform)

Below the spinous process of the 6th thoracic vertebra, in the supraspinal and interspinal ligaments.

This point attacks the diaphragm and can drain the body. It can also attack the spine and the central nervous system directly.

The heart may also be injured from a strong strike and can lead to cardiac arrest if severe enough.

Energetically, this point may disrupt the communication between the Shen and the mind leading to confusion.

Activation angle: 45°

GV-11: *Shendao* (Spirit's Path)

Located below the spinous process of the 5th thoracic vertebra.

The spine may be injured from a strong attack. Some say that it can lead to mental problems later in life.

Activation angle: 45°

GV-12: *Shenzhu* (Body's Pillar)

Below the spinous process of the 3rd thoracic vertebra, in the supraspinal and interspinal ligaments.

This point is known to damage the lungs. It can lead to coughing and even asthmatic attacks.

Energetically, it can imbalance the energy of the whole body.

Activation angle: 45°

GV-13: *Taodao* (Way of Happiness)

Below the spinous process of the 1st thoracic vertebra, in the supraspinal and interspinal ligaments.

- Origin Point of the Governing Vessel
- Intersection Point of the Bladder

This point can be hazardous to the spinal column.

Activation angle: 45°

GV-14: *Dazhui* (Big Vertebra)

Between the spinous process of the 7th cervical and the 1st thoracic vertebra, in the supraspinal ligament. *Da* means "large" and *Zhui* means "vertebra." This point is below the prominence of the 7th cervical vertebra which is the largest of the vertebra.

- Origin Point of the Governing Vessel

- Intersection Point of the Small Intestine
- Intersection Point of the Large Intestine
- Nourishes the Blood
- Four Seas Point: Sea of Qi
- Associated with an Extraordinary Vessel of the Governing Vessel
- One of 36 Vital Points Listed in the Bubishi

When struck downward, the body often drains of energy, with a weakening of all the limbs and faintness. This can lead to knock out. Spinal injury can also result.

When struck upwards, an increase of energy is sent into the upper torso and can lead to confusion.

From a healing standpoint, finger pressure can be used to provide some energy to a person.

Activation angle: 45°

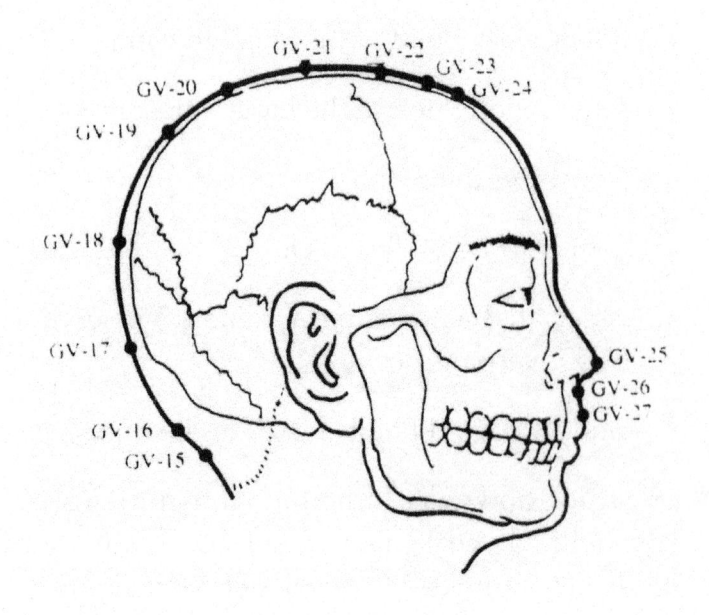

GV-15: *Yamen* (Door of Muteness)

At the midpoint of the nape, 0.5 cun above the natural hair line in the depression 0.5 cun below GV-16.

- Origin Point of the Governing Vessel
- Intersection Point of the Yang Linking Vessel
- Four Seas Point: Sea of Qi

This is a very dangerous point and may cause knock out and even death! Use extreme caution with this point.

Activation angle: 90°

GV-16: *Fengfu* (Wind's Dwelling)

Directly below the external occipital protuberance, in the depression between the trapezium muscles of both sides, 1 cun within the natural hairline at the back of the head.

- Origin Point of the Governing Vessel
- Intersection Point of the Yang Linking Vessel
- Stems counterflow
- Four Seas Point: Sea of Marrow
- Window of the Sky Point
- Associated with an Extraordinary Vessel of the Governing Vessel and Yang Linking Vessel
- One of 36 Vital Points Listed in the Bubishi

This point is slightly more dangerous than GV-15. It is located near the respiratory center in the rhombic depression at the 4th venticula.

It can produce knock out and even death. This point is connected with the Sea of Marrow and the brain.

It is an extremely dangerous point!

Activation angle: 45°

GV-17: *Naohu* (Brain's Household)

1.5 cun above GV-16, superior to the margin of the occipital protuberance.

This point is an extremely dangerous point!

It is situated close to foramen magnum, often referred to as the 'gate of the brain'.

It can easily produce knockout. Death may also occur from a hard strike.

Activation angle: 45°

GV-18: *Qiangjian* (Between Strength)

1.5 cun above GV-17, midway between GV-16 and GV-20.

A perpendicular strike may shock the brain and produce knock out with little pressure.

Activation angle: 45°

GV-19: *Houding* (Behind Top)

1.5 cun above GV-18, 1.5 cun behind GV-20 on the midline.

Little power is needed to drain the body of energy and attack the brain.

This point is fairly well protected by surrounding tissue, but a powerful strike can avert this.

Activation angle: 15°

GV-20: *Baihui* (Hundred Meetings)

7 cun above the posterior hairline, at the intersection of the median line at the vertex with a line drawn from the angle of the jaw through the apex of the ear and over to the other ear apex. In the galea aponeurotica, to the left and right of which are commonly found parietal foramen.

- Quiets the Spirit
- Lowers the blood pressure
- Stems counterflow

- Four Seas Point: Sea of Marrow

This point is often used in healing. From a Martial perspective, it is great for knock outs with a medium power strike. It is often attacked with a Palm Heel strike if you can get to it.

It can cause localized pain if struck lightly.

Activation angle: 15°

GV-21: *Qianding* (Before Top)

1.5 cun anterior to GV-20.

This point has the ability to traumatize the brain, causing the body to weaken, especially in the legs.

Attacked properly, it can even be fatal.

Activation angle: 45°

GV-22.: *Xinhui* (Fontanel's Meeting)

3 cun anterior to GV-20, 2 cun posterior to the anterior hairline.

- Associated with an Extraordinary Vessel of the Governing Vessel

- One of 36 Vital Points Listed in the Bubishi

This point can impair the vision and cause localized pain.

Activation angle: 15°

GV-23: *Shangzing* (Upper Star)

1 cun within the anterior hairline, 4 cun anterior to GV-20, on the midline. At the border between the left and right frontalis muscles.

- Stems counterflow

Comparable to GV-22 except that more energy may be drained.

Activation angle: 15°

GV-24: *Shenting* (Spirit's Hall)

On the midsagittal line of the head, 0.5 cun within the anterior hairline.

- Stems counterflow
- Associated with an Extraordinary Vessel of the Governing Vessel
- One of 36 Vital Points Listed in the Bubishi

This point may permanently harm the brain if struck hard enough.

The point is fairly well protected y surrounding bone and tissue.

Activation angle: 15°

GV-25: *Suliao* (Plain Seam)

At the tip of the nose.

This point is can injure the nose and cause bleeding.

Energetically, it is known to drain the energy, especially in the lungs.

Activation angle: 90°

GV-26: *Renzhong* (Philtrum)

Below the nose, a little above the midpoint of the philtrum (approximately one third the distance from the bottom of the nose to the top of the lip). In the orbicularis oris muscle.

- Origin Point of the Governing Vessel
- Intersection Point of the Stomach

- Intersection Point of the Large Intestine
- Stems counterflow
- Associated with an Extraordinary Vessel of the Governing Vessel
- One of 36 Vital Points Listed in the Bubishi

This point is often used in the healing arena to revive a person from shock. From a Martial perspective, it may induce shock when struck hard. Harder strikes may induce death! Lesser powerful strikes often cause knock out.

This point can imbalance the entire energetic system.

This is a very dangerous point!

Activation angle: 45°

GV-27: *Duiduan* (Exchange Terminus)

On the median tubercle of the upper lip, at the junction of the philtrum and the upper lip.

This point is relatively easy to strike and can produce shock. It can also knock teeth out if struck hard enough.

Activation angle: 45°

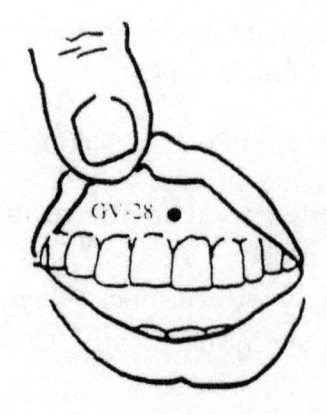

GV-28: *Yinjiao* (Gums Junction)

Between the upper lip and the upper labial gingiva, in the frenulum of the upper lip.

- Origin Point of the Governing Vessel
- Intersection Point of the Stomach

This point is more applicable to healing than Martial Arts since it is located inside the mouth.

Activation angle: 90°

Chapter 15

Yin Heel Vessel

Alternative Name(s)	Yin Motility Vessel
Chinese Name	*Yin Qiao Mai*
Paired Meridian(s)	N/A
Master Point	KI-6
Coupled Point	LU-7
Xi-Cleft Point	KI-8
Intersection Point(s)	KI-6, KI-8, BL-1

Table 15-1

Areas of effect

Medial aspect of lower extremities, genitals, abdomen, eyes, throat, chest, lungs, nervous, muscular skeletal, digestive and respiratory systems

Functions

- Controls the ascent of fluids and the descent of *Qi*.

Chapter 16

Yang Heel Vessel

Alternative Name(s)	Yang Motility Vessel
Chinese Name	*Yang Qiao Mai*
Paired Meridian(s)	Governing Vessel
Master Point	BL-62
Coupled Point	SI-3
Xi-Cleft Point	BL-59
Intersection Point(s)	BL-1, BL-59, BL-61, BL-62, GB-20, GB-29, SI-10, LI-15, LI-16, ST-1, ST-3, ST-4

Table 16-1

Areas of effect

Back, neck, eyes, nervous and muscular skeletal systems

Functions

- Issues of the eyes and/or face, eye pain (esp. inner canthus), redness and/or swelling, headache.
- Affects the lateral aspect of the lower limbs, numbness, weakness, and spasms.
- Excess Yang.
- Insomnia.

Pathway

Originates at BL-62 and travels behind the heel to BL-61. It continues up the calf to BL-59, up the lateral aspect of the leg to GB-29 and then up to the scapular region at SI-10. It continues to LI-15 and LI-16 and then travels to the face and connects with ST-4, ST-3, ST-1 and BL-1 where it meets with the BL, GV and Yin Heel Vessel. From here it travels over the head and terminates at GB-20.

Chapter 17

Yin Linking Vessel

Alternative Name(s)	Yin Motility Vessel
Chinese Name	*Yin Wei Mai*
Paired Meridian(s)	Penetrating Vessel
Master Point	PC-6
Coupled Point	SP-4
Xi-Cleft Point	KI-9
Intersection Point(s)	KI-9, LV-14, SP-13, SP-15, SP-16, CV-22, CV-23

Table 17-1

Areas of effect

Medial aspect of the lower limbs, nervous, cardiovascular, muscular skeletal and digestive systems.

Functions

- Affects the balance of Yin and Yang.

- Effects the Blood, Yin and Shen - blood circulation, heart pain, depression, blood deficiency headaches.

- Pain in the chest, back, middle and/or lower jiaos - abdominal distention, stomach ache, nausea, rectal prolapse.

Pathway

Originates at KI-9 and goes up along the medial aspect of the thigh into the abdomen where it enters the spleen meridian at SP-13, SP-15, and SP-16. It continues up to LV-14, enters the abdomen and continues upwards through the chest and throat. It then meets the Conception Vessel at CV-22 and CV-23.

Chapter 18

Yang Linking Vessel

Alternative Name(s)	N/A
Chinese Name	*Yang Wei Mai*
Paired Meridian(s)	Girdle Vessel
Master Point	TB-5
Coupled Point	GB-41
Xi-Cleft Point	GB-35
Intersection Point(s)	BL-63, SI-10, GV-15, GV-16, GB-13, GB-14, GB-15, GB-16, GB-17, GB-18, GB-19, GB-20, GB-21, GB-35, TB-15

Table 18-1

Areas of effect

Sides of the body, hips, joints, eyes, ears muscular skeletal and immune systems.

Functions

- Shao Yang level illnesses - alternating fever and chills.
- Pain and/or distention in the lumbar region.

Pathway

Originates at BL-63 and ascends along the GB meridian up the leg and sides of the body passing thru GB-35. It continues to BL-59 and up to the hip (GB-29). Then it continues along the lateral aspect of the body to LI-14 at the shoulder, to TB-13, TB-15 and to GB-21. It then travels down to SI-10, over to GV-15, GV-16 and then to GB-20. It continues downward along the GB meridian from GB-19 thru to GB-13 where it ends.

Chapter 19

Penetrating Vessel

Alternative Name(s)	N/A
Chinese Name	*Chong Mai*
Paired Meridian(s)	Yin Linking Vessel
Master Point	SP-4
Coupled Point	PC-6
Xi-Cleft Point	GB-35
Intersection Point(s)	KI-11, KI-12, KI-13, KI-14, KI-15, KI-16, KI-17, KI-18, KI-19, KI-20, KI-21, CV-1

Table 19-1

Areas of effect

Abdomen, thorax, genitals, Heart, inner thigh, reproductive, digestive and respiratory systems.

Functions

- "Sea of Blood" menstrual and/or reproductive issues, irregular menstruation, infertility.

- Physical and spiritual heart issues - Heart pain, depression.

- Balances rebellious *Qi* – hiccups.

- Abdominal stagnation.

- Respiratory issues - asthma.

Pathway

Originates in the ming men and passes through the uterus (in women) and down to CV-1. From here it emerges at ST-30 and continues upwards along the kidney meridian to KI-21. It then flows up the throat, encircles the mouth and continues up to the forehead.

A second branch flows from CV-1 inside the spine to the BL-23 area.

A third branch flows downwards towards the foot where it splits into two branches and follows the KI and SP meridians.

Chapter 20

Girdle Vessel

Alternative Name(s)	Belt Vessel
Chinese Name	*Dai Mai*
Paired Meridian(s)	Yang Linking Vessel
Master Point	GB-41
Coupled Point	TB-5
Xi-Cleft Point	N/A
Intersection Point(s)	GB-26, GB-27, GB-28, LV-13

Table 20-1

Areas of effect

lateral sides of the lumbar area gastrointestinal, female reproductive and muscular skeletal systems.

Functions

- Issues in the middle aspect of the body - abdominal distention, lumbar weakness, muscular weakness in the lumbar and/or lower extremities.

- Links the upper and lower halves of the body and helps to move *Qi* and Blood in the legs. Treats weakness in the legs, walking problems.

Pathway

Originates at LV-13, continues to and encircles GB-26 and LV-13 and then connects with GB-27 and GB-28.

Chapter 21

The Connecting Vessels

There are 16 connecting channels: 1 for each of the 12 meridians, a great connecting point for the ST as well as the SP in addition to their regular connecting points, 1 for the CV and 1 for the GV.

1. Lung separates at LU-7, follows the LU channel into the palm, spread through the thenar eminence and connects with the LI.

2. Large Intestine separates at LI-6, joins the LU meridian, ascends the arm going through LI-15 to the jaw where it divides, one branch going to the teeth and the other enters the ear.

3. Spleen separates at SP-4, connects with the ST meridian, ascends up the medial aspect of the leg and connects with the Stomach and intestines.

4. Spleen Great connecting vessel separates at SP-21, spreads through the chest and the lateral costal region.

5. Stomach separates at ST-40, joins the SP, ascends the leg and continues to the base of the neck where it joins the Qi of the other yang channels and terminates in the throat.

6. Stomach Great connecting vessel is sometimes seen as a throbbing below the left breast and connects with the LU.

7. Heart separates at HT-5, joins the SI, follows the HT meridian to the HT and continues to the root of the tongue and into the eyes.

8. Small Intestine separates at SI-7, joins the HT, ascends the arm at connects with LI-15.

9. Kidney separates at KI-5, encircles the heel and enters internally connecting with the BL, follows up to a point below the heart and travels posteriorly spreading into the lumbar region.

10. Bladder separates at BL-58, connects with the KI meridian.

11. Pericardium separates at PC-6, connects with the TB, ascends along the TH and connects with the PC and the HT.

12. Triple Heater separates at TB-5 travels up the posterior aspect of the arm and joins the PC in the chest.

13. Liver separates at LV-5, connects with the GB and travels up the legs to the genitals.

14. Gall Bladder separates at GB-37, connects with the LV, descends and disperses over the dorsum of the foot.

15. Conception Vessel separates at CV-15, descends and disperses over the abdomen.

16. Governing Vessel separates at GV-1, ascends bilaterally along the sides of the spine to the base of the neck, and spreads out over the occiput.

Appendix

36 Vital Points of the Bubishi		
Eyes	GB-3	LI-4
Ears	GB-24	LI-10
BL-40	GB-31	LU-3
BL-43	GV-1	LU-8
BL-51	GV-14	LV-3
BL-62	GV-16	LV-11
CV-1	GV-22	LV-13
CV-4	GV-24	ST-9
CV-15	GV-26	ST-12
CV-18	HT-1	SI-16
CV-22	HT-5	TB-2
CV-24	KI-6	TB-17

Meridian	Accumulating Point
Lung	LU-6
Large Intestine	LI-7
Stomach	ST-34
Spleen	SP-8
Heart	HT-6
Small Intestine	SI-6
Bladder	BL-63
Kidney	KI-4
Pericardium	PC-4
Triple Burner	TB-7
Gall Bladder	GB-36
Liver	LV-6
Extra Meridians	**Accumulating Point**
Yin Linking Vessel	KI-9
Yang Linking Vessel	GB-35
Yin Heel Vessel	KI-8
Yang Heel Vessel	BL-59

Meridian	Alarm Point
Lung	LU-1
Large Intestine	ST-25
Stomach	CV-12
Spleen	LV-13
Heart	CV-14
Small Intestine	CV-4
Bladder	CV-3
Kidney	GB-25
Pericardium	CV-15
Triple Burner	CV-5
Gall Bladder	GB-24
Liver	LV-14

Meridian	Associated Point
Lung	BL-13
Pericardium	BL-14
Heart	BL-15
(Governing Vessel)	(BL-16)
Liver	BL-18
Gall Bladder	BL-19
Spleen	BL-20
Stomach	BL-21
Triple Burner	BL-22
Kidney	BL-23
Large Intestine	BL-25
Small Intestine	BL-27
Bladder	BL-28

Meridian	Cleft-xi Point
Lung	LU-6
Large Intestine	LI-7
Stomach	ST-34
Spleen	SP-8
Heart	HT-6
Small Intestine	SI-6
Bladder	BL-63
Kidney	KI-5
Pericardium	PC-4
Triple Burner	TB-7
Gall Bladder	GB-36
Liver	LV-6
Yang Motility	BL-59
Yin Motility	KI-8
Yang Linking	GB-35
Yin Linking	KI-9

Extra Meridians	Confluence
Yin Linking Vessel	PC-6
Yang Linking Vessel	TB-5
Yin Heel Vessel	KI-6
Yang Heel Vessel	BL-62
Penetrating Vessel	SP-4
Girdling Vessel	GB-41
Conception Vessel	LU-7
Governing Vessel	SI-3

Meridian	Connecting-luo
Lung & Large Intestine	LU-7 & LI-6
Stomach & Spleen	ST-40 & SP-4
Heart & Small Intestine	HT-5 & SI-7
Bladder & Kidney	BL-58 & KI-6
Pericardium & Triple Burner	PC-6 & TB-5
Gall Bladder & Liver	GB-37 & LV-5
Conception Vessel &	CV-15 & GV-1

Meridian	"Destructive" Meridian	Destructive Point
Lung	Fire	LU-10
Large Intestine	Fire	LI-5
Stomach	Wood	ST-43
Spleen	Wood	SP-1
Heart	Water	HT-3
Small Intestine	Water	SI-2
Bladder	Earth	BL-54
Kidney	Earth	KI-5
Pericardium	Water	PC-3
Triple	Water	TB-2
Gall Bladder	Metal	GB-44
Liver	Metal	LV-4

Meridian	Entry Point
Lung	LU-1
Large Intestine	LI-4
Stomach	ST-1
Spleen	SP-1
Heart	HT-1
Small Intestine	SI-1
Bladder	BL-1
Kidney	KI-1
Pericardium	PC-1
Triple Burner	TB-1
Gall Bladder	GB-1
Liver	LV-1

Meridian	Exit Point
Lung	LU-7
Large Intestine	LI-20
Stomach	ST-42
Spleen	SP-21
Heart	HT-9
Small Intestine	SI-19
Bladder	BL-67
Kidney	KI-22
Pericardium	PC-8
Triple Burner	TB-23
Gall Bladder	GB-41
Liver	LV-14

Extraordinary Vessel Pairings	
Yin Motility Vessel	Conception Vessel
Yang Motility Vessel	Governing Vessel
Yin Linking Vessel	Penetrating Vessel
Yang Linking Vessel	Girdle Vessel

Extraordinary Vessel	Master Point	Coupled Point
Conception Vessel	LU-7	KI-6
Governing Vessel	SI-3	BL-62
Penetrating Vessel	SP-4	PC-6
Girdle Vessel	GB-41	TB-5
Yin Heel Vessel	KI-6	LU-7
Yang Heel Vessel	BL-62	SI-3
Yin Linking Vessel	PC-6	SP-4
Yang Linking Vessel	TB-5	GB-41

Five Element Points

YIN	Element	Wood	Fire	Earth	Metal	Water
Lung	Metal	LU-11	LU-10	LU-9	LU-8	LU-5
Heart	Fire	HT-9	HT-8	HT-7	HT-4	HT-3
Pericardium	Fire	PC-9	PC-8	PC-7	PC-5	PC-3
Liver	Wood	LV-1	LV-2	LV-3	LV-4	LV-8
Spleen	Earth	SP-1	SP-2	SP-3	SP-5	SP-9
Kidney	Water	KI-1	KI-2	KI-5	KI-7	KI-10

Five Element Points

YANG	Element	Wood	Fire	Earth	Metal	Water
Large Intestine	Metal	LI-3	LI-5	LI-11	LI-1	LI-2
Small Intestine	Fire	SI-3	SI-5	SI-8	SI-1	SI-2
Triple Burner	Fire	TB-3	TB-6	TB-10	TB-1	TB-2
Gall Bladder	Wood	GB-41	GB-38	GB-34	GB-44	GB-43
Stomach	Earth	ST-43	ST-41	ST-36	ST-45	ST-44
Bladder	Water	BL-65	BL-60	BL-54	BL-67	BL-66

Sea	Four Seas Point
Sea of Nourishment	ST-30 & ST-36
Sea of Blood	BL-11, ST-37, and ST-39
Sea of Energy	CV-17, BL-10, ST-9, and CV-6
Sea of Marrow	GV-20 & GV-16

Meridian	Horary Point
Lung	LU-8
Large Intestine	LI-1
Stomach	ST-36
Spleen	SP-3
Heart	HT-8
Small Intestine	SI-5
Bladder	BL-66
Kidney	KI-10
Pericardium	PC-8
Triple Burner	TB-6
Gall Bladder	GB-41
Liver	LV-1

Action	Intersection Point	Intersecting Meridian
Enhance Fire	GB-1	Small Intestine &
	GB-3	Triple Burner
	GB-4	Triple Burner
	GB-5	Triple Burner
	GB-6	Triple Burner
	GB-14	Triple Burner
	GB-21	Small Intestine Triple Burner
Enhance Metal	ST-3	Large Intestine
	ST-4	Large Intestine
Enhance Wood	None	None
Enhance Earth	None	None
Enhance Water	LI-14	Bladder

Meridian	"Insulting" Meridian	Insulting Point
Lung	Wood	LU-11
Large Intestine	Wood	LI-3
Stomach	Water	ST-44
Spleen	Water	SP-9
Heart	Metal	HT-4
Small Intestine	Metal	SI-1
Bladder	Fire	BL-60
Kidney	Fire	KI-2
Pericardium	Metal	PC-5
Triple	Metal	TB-1
Gall Bladder	Earth	GB-34
Liver	Earth	LV-3

Meridian	Sedation Point
Lung	LU-5
Large Intestine	LI-2, LI-3
Stomach	ST-45
Spleen	SP-5
Heart	HT-7
Small Intestine	SI-8
Bladder	BL-65
Kidney	KI-1, KI-2
Pericardium	PC-7
Triple Burner	TB-10
Gall Bladder	GB-38
Liver	LV-2

Meridian	Shokanten Point
Lung	LV-13
Large Intestine	ST-27
Stomach	ST-27
Spleen	LV-13
Heart	KI-16
Small Intestine	KI-12
Bladder	KI-12
Kidney	KI-16
Pericardium	LV-14 and KI-19
Triple Burner	ST-25 and KI-21
Gall Bladder	ST-25 and KI-21
Liver	LV-14 and KI-19

Meridian	Source Point
Lung	LU-9
Large Intestine	LI-4
Stomach	ST-42
Spleen	SP-3
Heart	HT-7
Small Intestine	SI-3
Bladder	BL-64
Kidney	KI-5
Pericardium	PC-7
Triple Burner	TB-4
Gall Bladder	GB-40
Liver	LV-3

Meridian	Tonification Point
Lung	LU-9
Large Intestine	LI-11
Stomach	ST-41
Spleen	SP-2
Heart	HT-9
Small Intestine	SI-3
Bladder	BL-67
Kidney	KI-7
Pericardium	PC-9
Triple Burner	TB-3
Gall Bladder	GB-43
Liver	LV-8

Meridian	Uniting-he Point
Stomach	ST-36
Large Intestine	ST-37
Small Intestine	ST-39
Gall Bladder	GB-34
Bladder	BL-40
Triple Burner	BL-39

"Window of the Sky" Points
ST-9
TB-16
LU-3
GV-15
SI-17
LI-18
BL-10
CV-22
SI-16
PC-1

Bibliography

Acubriefs, http://www.acubriefs.com. Helpful for channel pathways and functions.

Ellis, Andrew, Nigel Wiseman and Ken Boss, *Fundamentals of Chinese Acupuncture*, Brookline, Massachusetts: Paradigm Publications, 1989.

Ellis, Andrew, Nigel Wiseman and Ken Boss, *Grasping the Wind*, Brookline, Massachusetts: Paradigm Publications, 1989.

Guardian Dragon Discussion Forum, http://groups.msn.com/GuardianDragon/meridians.msnw. Very helpful for point locations and even results of strikes to the points.

Mann, Felix, Acupuncture, *The Ancient Chinese Art of Healing and How It Works Scientifically*, New York: Vintage Books, 1962.

Moneymaker, Rick, *Torite-Jutsu Reference Manual*, Chattanooga, Tennessee: Northshore Communications, 1997.

Moneymaker, Rick, Master's Series Notes.

About the Author

Master Michael Patrick has over twenty years of experience in the Martial Arts and holds Master-level certifications in the arts of Torite Jutsu and Isshin-ryu Karate. He is one of the foremost authorities on the application of Martial Science and its continued development. In 1999, he was inducted into the World Martial Arts Hall of Fame as the Instructor of the Year. He has also been inducted into the United Karate Systems of America Hall of Fame.

He has produced, edited, and been featured in a series of Martial Arts instructional videos for Dragon Society International. He is a contributing author to the *Torite Jutsu Reference* Manual. His articles have been published internationally in Martial Arts magazines in Europe, such as *Martial Arts Illustrated*, and on the world wide web.

His association with the Dragon Society International (DSI) opened his eyes to a world of information on the advanced concepts of Martial Science that he had previously never known existed. He was a part of an elite research group within the DSI. Much of the work presented here was the result of that research. Until now, much of this information has not been publicly released.

He attends and instructs seminars sponsored by Dragon Society International world-wide on a regular basis.

Master Patrick is a direct student of Grand Masters Rick Moneymaker and Tom Muncy, founders of Dragon

Society International. He is also a student of Grand Master Allen Wheeler in Isshin-ryu Karate.

He has trained numerous students in the fields of Law Enforcement, Fugitive Recovery, and Martial Arts.

He has a wonderful family with three children, Mark, Kayla, and Kristopher, along with a lovely wife, Kasi. He is very active with his family and church.

Master Patrick is always available for seminars, which receive outstanding reviews. He is considered the "teacher's teacher." He is well known for the depth of detail that he provides and his willingness to share it.

If you are interested in learning more about having Master Patrick provide training at your school, seminar, or event, please contact him at:

Mike Patrick
130 West Bernard Avenue
Greeneville, TN 37743

(423) 639-KICK

www.patrickskarate.com
mike@patrickskarate.com

If you would like to learn more about Dragon Society International or to become a member, please visit our Web site at: www.dragonsociety.com.

Special Thanks to My Beloved Family

You all are awesome!